Performing Shakespeare

A Way to Learn

Mary Hartman, Shakespeare & Company Director of Education Programs, conducting a Workshop.

Performing Shakespeare

A Way to Learn

Robert Sugarman

Author of *Circus for Everyone:
Circus Learning Around the World*

Mountainside Press

Copyright © 2005 by Robert Sugarman
Foreword copyright © 2005 by Kristin Linklater
All rights reserved.
This book may not be reproduced in whole or in part in any form without permission in writing from the publisher, except by a reviewer who wishes to quote brief passages in connection with a review written for inclusion in a magazine, newspaper, or broadcast.

Book design and layout by Shakespeare, Inc.

10 9 8 7 6 5 4 3 2 1

Library of Congress Cataloging-in-Publication Data

Library of Congress Control Number: 2005924079

ISBN 0-9708693-4-7

Mountainside Press
P.O. Box 407
Shaftsbury, VT 05262
Phone: (802) 447-76179
FAX: (802) 447-2611
mntnside@sover.net
www.mountainsidepress.com

Cover photo credits: clockwise from upper left, students of Shakespeare & Company in A Midsummer Night's Dream; Caitlin Ellison, student of Lois Burdett, photo courtesy Robin Wilhelm; Hobart Shakespeareans, photo courtesy Kurt Ingham.

In memory of Marvin Sugarman

1916-2003

"He was a man, take him for all in all;
I shall not look upon his like again."
—*Hamlet*

Contents

Foreword by Kristin Linklater . . . . *ix*

Acknowledgements . . . . *xiii*

About this Book . . . . *xv*

I: Shakespeare and Young People 3

II: Four Approaches. 11

    Beginnings 11
    Lois Burdett and the Hamlet School 11
    Stephen Haff and the Real People Theater. 18
    Rafe Esquith and the Hobart Shakespeareans 21
    Kevin Coleman and Mary Hartman and
    Shakespeare & Company. 24

    The Process. 28
    The Hamlet School 28
    The Real People Theater. 33
    The Hobart Shakespeareans. 41
    Shakespeare & Company. 52

    Common Denominators 63

III. Your Program 67

    Approaching the Work........................ 67
    Making Theatre 69
    Directing Shakespeare 71
    Engaging the Students 75
    Moving towards Performance 78
    Moving Ahead 82
    Preparing for Performance..................... 85

IV. A Hypothetical Production of
A Midsummer Night's Dream 99

Final Thoughts 131

Appendix 135

Endnotes 163

Bibliography.................................... 167

Index... 171

Foreword
by Kristin Linklater

A Way to Learn is the subtitle of Robert Sugarman's book *Performing Shakespeare*. This suggests that in performing Shakespeare's plays young people may find out more than their classroom education offers. Strangely, in a culture that is flooded by video games, reality TV and the ever-expanding computer and electronic entertainment universe, there is abundant anecdotal evidence of the unique educational and healing power of Shakespeare. Shakespeare performed, enacted, spoken. Wherever there are programs that bring the experience of playing Shakespeare into schools there are stories of improved learning focus, diminished delinquencies and enhanced appreciation of life potential. Although there is currently little institutional recognition of these valuable additions to the learning process, I believe that the anecdotal evidence will eventually influence educational policies and integrated support will emerge.

It is not only in schools that Shakespeare's plays wreak small and larger miracles without adequate acknowledgement. Shakespeare programs in prisons and juvenile detention cen-

---

Kristin Linklater is the author of *Freeing the Natural Voice* and *Freeing Shakespeare's Voice*. The Linklater technique is one of the leading methodologies of voice training in the theater today. A co-founder of Shakespeare & Company in Lenox, MA, she has taught at New York University Graduate Theatre Program and Emerson College and is currently Professor of Theatre Arts at Columbia University.

ters are woefully under-valued and under-supported in relation to the enlightenment they bring to rehabilitation efforts. How does this playwright from another time and another place, bearing the stigma of elitist academia, speaking in a hard, old, almost foreign tongue, maintain his practical and effective power across socio-economic and educational boundaries? Certainly part of his power comes from archetypal stories that need to be told over and over again because humanity doesn't change very much and we human beings need to tell and re-tell our repetitive tales: of woes, of loves, hates and jealousies, of weakness and ambition, of occasional redemptions and manifold punishments, of forgiveness and transformation. But it is the language in which these tales are told that makes the miracles happen. The root of the word 'language' is the same as for 'tongue'. It's a hard but lively old tongue that tells these tales. And it is our mother-tongue. When children (of any age) wrap their tongues around Shakespeare's language their brains awaken to a tough mother-love that says "work hard, but play as hard as you work". Words challenge the imagination and imagination engenders action. That is how actors make plays. When children eat these words and digest them they create rich nutrition for their imaginations; and then they find their own words to explain their own lives and they can invent their futures with a vocabulary to support their experiences and their dreams. Without a language to describe their largest hopes children dwindle into a depleted mental state, and, all too often, mere bottom-line subsistence.

There are probably hundreds of thousands of Shakespeare lovers in this country who want to pass on their passion to young people and share with them the joy that has uplifted their lives. But how are they to go about it? I would suggest that almost anywhere in the country there are enough "bardolators" to form a formidably persuasive action group that could infiltrate and transform a local community in one way or another through Shakespeare's plays either read aloud or fully performed. But, it is certainly true that enthusiasm is not enough. Some forms of expertise, some formulae, some methods of approach seem essential to turn passion into practice. Robert Sugarman has identified four programs, out of many that are successful, to illustrate four very different ways in which Shakespeare can be brought to vibrant life within or around (and not necessarily with curricular support) the school system. Here are strategies and tactics, points of view and down-to-earth accounts of how personal commitment (perhaps with a touch of fanaticism) can surmount all sorts of obstacles and bring profound experiences of creativity and artistic satisfaction into the lives of young people.

Lois Burdett says "I don't concentrate on performance. What I feel is most important is the writing. Then the performance comes....I use Shakespeare as a means to an end...When we were studying *The Winter's Tale*, one little girl wrote, 'Leontes' eyes were like overheated flames, his cheeks were red as a lobster, grabbing the scroll like a child with no manners he screamed 'Lies, lies'. A hush fell over the crowd. We all wept like wilting flowers. Hermione's brows slid down to her eyes." She does Shakespeare with second and third graders. Stephen Haff, working with inner city Brooklyn teenagers says "Rewriting the script is their way of making it their own. And they retitled it *Hamlet, Prince of Brooklyn*....They are a feisty group and rehearsals aren't always easy. I chose these kids because they are feisty...It's a matter not of telling them 'Don't do that,' but saying, 'How angry you are right now. Use that.' Reminding them that emotions are very good—they're very human. It's the choices you make about how to use them.'" Rafe Esquith, working with fourth and fifth graders says "They are a team. And they function well together. People are amazed when they come to the show with all the kids onstage, backstage and behind the scenes and there are no adults at all….We have a real kickass rock and roll band and we do 10 to 15 songs during the Shakespeare play…We have about 30 songs for *Hamlet* …we'll get it down to 12…when you have sixty or more kids in a play…I don't want to have [them] spending all that time holding a spear." Shakespeare & Company's Kevin Coleman says "You don't have to be able to read to do Shakespeare. We find that the kid who can't read memorizes faster than anyone…When that kid gets up to play Romeo, there's another kid behind him who can read who feeds him a line at a time….The Romeo takes it in from hearing it". The four very different approaches stimulate ideas for other strategies and tactics, exercises and experiments.

From Robert Sugarman's own extensive background in theatre comes an encouraging voice that suggests ways to move through the difficulties of introducing Shakespeare performance to young people and arrive at the immense satisfaction of seeing the results. In his book he has assembled reports, strategies and tools that can help make passionate bardolatry practical and effective.

Acknowledgements

The orientation to theatrical performance that informs this book developed over many years. The two years I spent as Stage Manager at The Actors Studio in New York City introduced me to Lee Strasberg's belief that actors can bring truth, not just the naturalistic truth that is often identified with Strasberg's work, but all aspects of human experience to the stage. He taught me that a path to this was relaxation and a focus on sensory detail. The subsequent two years I spent in the Actors Studio Playwrights and Directors Unit gave me the opportunity to have director Elia Kazan lead the discussion of two plays I had written. His focus on the importance of a play's event helped my playwriting, my directing and my understanding of theatrical performance. Joan Littlewood, at the Theatre Workshop in London, showed me how dynamic a stage ensemble can be when actors truly trust what they are doing.

Doing graduate work at Hunter College, I benefited from the late Prof. Wallace Gray's insight into directing and I allude to him in the text. Prof. Vera Mowry Roberts instilled in me a lifelong fascination with theatre history.

I wish I could mention all the Shakespearean productions I have seen in this country, Canada and England. When doing doctoral research in London in 1968-1969, I saw all of the productions at the Royal Shakespeare Company, then under the direction of Trevor Nunn and Terry Hands, and had the opportunity to interview Mr. Hands about them. During the last twenty years I have attended most of the productions at the Stratford Festival in Canada and Shakespeare & Company in Massachusetts. And there have been many others. All these performances broadened my vision of what is possible when bringing Shakespeare to the stage.

I thank all of those doing Shakespeare with young people who shared their ideas and their productions with me. As I organized this book, I found it useful to focus on four: Lois Burdett and her second graders in the Hamlet School in Stratford, Ontario; Steven Haff and the high school members of the Real People Theater in Brooklyn; Rafe Esquith and his fifth grade Hobart Shakespeareans in Los Angeles; and Mary Hartman and Kevin Coleman and the grammar and high school programs of Shakespeare & Company. Those people generously answered endless queries from me. I also thank those from the groups not included in the book who contributed to my understanding of what is involved when doing Shakespeare with young people. Notable among these are Catharine Hall-Schor in the North Bennington, Vermont Graded School; Jessica Howard at Hiland Hall School in Shaftsbury, Vermont; Daryl Kenny at Mount Anthony Union High School in Bennington, Vermont; Pat Quigley, Education Director at the Stratford Festival in Ontario; Sean Fagan and his Shakespeare's Clowns at the Robert C. Parker School in Troy, New York; and Dic Wheeler and Marcella Trowbridge of the Summer Shakespeare Academy in Middletown, Connecticut. I also thank Kristin Linklater for her generous foreword.

I thank my son Paul for his passion for Shakespeare and the First Folio. His work with the Instant Shakespeare Company in New York City has involved and enriched our family. I also thank him for designing this book. I thank his wife Maren, a fine director, who encouraged me to simplify my presentation. Finally, I gratefully acknowledge the contribution of my wife Sally who has had great insights into the productions we have seen together and has enthusiastically supported this venture.

Robert Sugarman

About this Book

This book is for those who want to enrich the experience young people have performing Shakespeare's plays. It is also for those who have yet to undertake Shakespearean performance with youngsters. To bring Shakespeare's plays to life, it helps to place the participants in the kind of performing space Shakespeare's actors employed. Sets, no more essential now than they were in Shakespeare's time, are de-emphasized. The book eschews the picture frame proscenium stage that evolved as artificial lighting made "realistic" settings possible. It advocates a more direct relationship between audiences and actors than prosceniums allow. It proposes performing Shakespeare in workshops before preparing presentations with their daunting deadlines. Finally, it describes the learning that can accrue to young people who perform Shakespeare—learning about language, imagination, hard work and cooperation as well as learning about the complexity of the lives that lie around and before them.

The first chapter presents a rationale for undertaking Shakespearean production with young people. The second describes four programs that have had success. The third suggests ways to develop or improve your own program. A background in theatre is useful, but two of the programs examined were created by people with no theatre background. What all the directors share is a passion to help young people experience Shakespeare's work. The chapter explores ways a director can help actors bring any playwright's script to life by creating the experience that makes the playwright's words, and the actions of which they are part, inevitable.

The final chapter demonstrates the kind of questions and concerns that confront a director and actors when creating a production. To do this, the chapter considers a hypothetical production of *A Midsummer Night's Dream.*

Research for this book has shown the author how meaningful the work can be. He hopes to share with you his conviction that performing Shakespeare is a unique way for young people to learn.

I:
Shakespeare and Young People

Lois Burdett's second graders at Stratford, Ontario's Hamlet School

The cast of Los Angeles' Hobart Elementary School *Hamlet*.

Kevin Coleman, center, leads participants in Shakespeare & Company's Fall Festival Common Class in performance

SHAKESPEARE AND YOUNG PEOPLE

An unfortunate aura of elitism is often associated with the arts. Shakespeare's plays were not elite or "literature" when first presented. They were popular entertainment. Today the plays are not only for the elite, but for students who need strategies and a sense of their own worth that can help them break out of constrained situations. The greater the need, the greater the importance of this work.

Young people should not *study* Shakespeare's plays, they should *do* them. As educators prepare students for standardized tests, students' out of school hours are often spent in isolation with the media as companions. Young people need the visceral, communal, challenging experience Shakespearean production can provide.

Schools and communities promote competitive sports because they are said to teach leadership, cooperation and physical fitness while contributing to school or community spirit. In ghetto areas basketball is exalted as a way out of deprived circumstances although less than one per cent of the participants ever earn the scholarships that could lead to higher education.[i] Although schools and communities share the glory and anguish of their teams' achievements, only the athletic elites play the games.

All young people can participate in non-competitive Shakespeare programs which also create spirit. Although the 400 year old language can be daunting, committed directors can use it to lead students to enrich their own language. Entering Shakespeare's magical, violent and lyrical world helps young people cope better with their own world's strangeness. The passions in the plays are not unfamiliar to young people and are pedagogically more valuable than the desire of an athletic team to destroy an opponent. As for fitness, students doing Shakespeare must fight, dance and sing.

An enemy of meaningful Shakespearean performances is the tradition of Victorian gentility that so often emasculates them. A Shakespeare production should be as vital as the world it came from. This means focusing on the event and the language of the plays, not on scenery and costumes. Since all productions have limited budgets and time, the emphasis is best kept on the acting. Rather than work on a proscenium stage which distances actors from the audience and calls for settings to fill the picture frame arch, programs are best served by moving into a space that audiences and actors share. Lighting? Why? Shakespeare's plays were done in daylight with the audience lit as much as the actors. It is fine if costumes and lighting are available to enhance productions, but they should never be primary considerations. When a situation demands work on a proscenium stage, the focus must be on the acting which will be compromised by the confrontational distance prosceniums establish between actors and audiences. Soliloquies that are awkward when breaking the fourth wall illusion of a proscenium, are simple and direct when the audience is accepted as part of the performing situation.

Shakespeare's World

So much was new in the Elizabethan world. When Shakespeare was a child, Catholicism was England's state religion and medieval plays were performed on the magic *platea*—the bare stage that could be anywhere from creation to Hell. On it, actors "out Heroded Herod." When Shakespeare was adult, the land was Protestant. Spies sought out followers of the old religion. Personal belief and loyalty to the sovereign were often at odds. It is important for young people to learn that Shakespeare was a real person with a wife and children, one of whom died, and a career that often kept him from them. He lived for the most part in London, the center of a new nation that had defeated the mighty Spanish Armada. The very language was new. Words were created and spelled with enthusiasm. It was a youthful time even as it was a time of filth, public executions, disease, bear baiting, murders and duels. Shakespeare built his dramatic fictions from that world on the old *platea* no more burdened by constraints of time or place than were the plays he had seen as a child.

As today's young people recreate Shakespeare's plays, they can share their energy with Shakespeare and his time. In the extravagance and volatile imagery of Shakespeare's language and in the extreme actions—swordplay, death, heroism, bawdy humor, wit, triumph, humiliation—young actors find things they can understand from their own experience. If the work is done with the sense of joy that characterizes the productions discussed in this book, young actors are able to explore the adult world that lies before them.

Those doing Shakespeare find themselves in a world where there are no correct answers. The characters they portray are—like life—ambiguous. Aaron in *Titus Andronicus* and Iago in *Othello* are atypical Shakespearean characters because they are so overwhelmingly evil—close to characters in medieval plays. Most Shakespearean characters show another side. Richard III does terrible things, but is a charmer. In *King Lear,* the pleasure Edmond takes in his evil machinations is engaging.

Any acting performance is shaped by the actor. The character assumes the actor's shape and voice. The uniqueness that can place a youngster outside the social and athletic norms may be the basis of remarkable performances. Taking possession of one's uniqueness in something as public as a production or a workshop helps develop the self assurance young people need. This carries over into life where the non-individuated identities fostered by video games, films, television and the celebrity rock culture are pervasive. How much better when young people confront the real experiences of Shakespeare's fictions with their own personas.

Youngsters must inhabit the plays before they analyze them. Instead the plays are best approached through games and improvisations. The actors should learn about the world in which the plays developed. The highly charged language that will in time enable them to express themselves must not be a deterrent as they approach the plays. That language is so much richer than that with which they are familiar, it will choke them if they do not approach it slowly. The plays must be *played*!

Participating in the performance of Shakespeare's plays can be a life enhancing experience. For some young people it becomes life changing as they engage with their potential for meaningful learning for the first time. Such discoveries can lead them to stay in school and pursue higher education which they had not previously considered. For people whose minds and bodies are transforming, engaging with the limitless possibilities of the Elizabethan spirit as expressed by the most remarkable writer our language has produced offers a new sense of the richness of their own world. This is especially so if their world is circumscribed by economic, racial or ethnic constraints or an educational system that has been more custodial than teaching. When Shakespearean production is done well, it is visceral as well as a stimulating intellectual activity. Mastering the difficulties is deeply satisfying and does much to confirm one's sense of one's own worth at a time when young people need affirmation based on genuine achievement.

Just because a play was written by Shakespeare does not guarantee that performing it will be valuable for the actors. It is not enough for youngsters to be thrust into Shakespearean productions they do not understand even when manipulated by directors into work that is impressive on stage.

The better programs are those in which Shakespeare is done *through* young people. The weaker, those in which Shakespeare is done *to* them. This is not to say that the weaker programs have no value. Just as in a poorly taught class, some students will get the message. For others, participating in Shakespeare productions that are less than ideal can be useful. Such productions allow young people to present themselves to family and friends as achievers—as persons in their own right. In such cases Shakespeare is being used for other—albeit valuable—ends. How much better when participants are enriched by meaningful engagement with Shakespeare's plays.

Doing Shakespeare is not a matter of age. It depends on how the work has been presented to those doing it. Canadian second graders in Lois Burdett's class in Stratford, Ontario encounter Shakespeare as a way to explore language. Their exploration leads them to create their own figurative speeches and present fully understood Shakespearean presentations. Stephen Haff works with high school students, many of whom speak English as a second language, in an extracurricular program in the Bushwick section of Brooklyn, New York. Working with them, Haff recreates Shakespeare's plays in an amalgam of "Street, Spanish and Shakespeare" that enables the students to engage with the plays. Rafe Esquith, working with fifth graders in a Los Angeles area where English is often a second language, spends a year preparing students to do uncut versions of the plays augmented by rock music they perform themselves. Shakespeare & Company in Lenox Massachusetts has programs that involve grammar and high school students in experiencing Shakespeare in unconventional ways to create productions.

In each of these programs, students make Shakespeare

their own without diminishing the richness of the scripts' language. Burdett's program and those of Shakespeare & Co. are sources of pride for the schools in which they operate. Haff and Esquith's afterschool programs are almost subversive in their institutions. Esquith funds his efforts privately and is at best tolerated by his colleagues and administrators in the classroom where his performances take place. Haff's productions are presented outside the school and now his Real People Theatre has secured its own performing space. If administrators of schools where exemplary programs take place are not supportive, it suggests that the value of such programs is not widely understood.

It is worth noting that in Stratford, Ontario, home of Ms. Burdett's program and Lenox, Massachusetts, home of Shakespeare & Company, professional Shakespearean productions have become a vital economic force in the communities. Sadly, in the areas where Haff and Esquith work, Shakespeare is just a long dead writer. Haff's students are sometimes harassed by their peers for doing work after school for which they are not paid. One Haff student responded saying, "When you're still flipping hamburgers, I'll be acting somewhere." Whether or not students become professional actors, there is value in doing Shakespeare. By participating, youngsters develop a life enhancing understanding of art, a work ethic and a sense of their own possibilities.

II:
Four Approaches

Four Approaches

This chapter looks at four successful Shakespeare programs. It considers how the programs began and how young people begin their involvement with the programs. It then explores the way these programs operate. Finally, it attempts to find common denominators in the work.

Beginnings

Lois Burdett—Stratford, Ontario

Stratford, Ontario was a major Canadian railroad center. When that ended, Tom Patterson and other town fathers sought another activity that would revive the community. They considered establishing a hockey center, but noting the town's name, explored the possibility of creating a Shakespeare Festival. Funds were raised to send Patterson to New York where Laurence Olivier was performing to see if he had any suggestions. Olivier did. He suggested British director Tyrone Guthrie who, intrigued by the idea, came to Stratford and established the Festival in a tent in 1953 with Alec Guinness as his leading man in a production of *Richard III*. The festival flourished and has transformed the community.

The Festival now has four theatres and a reputation for producing excellent work. It has become a destination for theatre-goers from around the world. The British actors who first appeared have been replaced by Canadians and the impact of the Festival on theatre throughout North America has been profound. It is not surprising that if a second grade Shakespeare program were to develop anywhere, it might be in Stratford. However, it was teacher Lois Burdett. who made the program happen. She has written a number of books based on her work[ii] and conducts workshops that introduce teachers to the methods she developed that lead her students from the three and four word declarative statements they write when they enter her class to rich figurative writing. She described what she does.

> When I began—almost thirty years ago—I didn't have any intention of doing Shakespeare. I had this little group of kids sitting around me on the carpet and I said, "There's a play called Hamlet by William Shakespeare." They had no idea what I was talking about. One little girl told me her mother met William Shakespeare before he died. It evolved from there. Making that connection with a historical figure got me going. Initially the school was surprised because there weren't classes of seven-year-olds doing Shakespearean plays. It was like forbidden territory. As soon as the school saw the kind of writing that was being produced and the amazing changes in the kids, they were thrilled. So now they come and ask, "What play are we doing?" In a lot of cases the children changed the negative opinions the parents had about Shakespeare because the parents were impressed with what they saw.
>
> How it goes depends on the class and on the

year. For example, a few years ago I had a grade 2 and then I had a 2-3. Those threes I had already taught in grade 2. They came in the first day of school begging me to do Macbeth. As soon as we finished, they wanted to do another. So it just took over the whole year. Right now I'm doing a line from a play and they're writing poetry with it. So we're not doing a play, but they're writing some beautiful similes. One year we went to see *Fiddler on the Roof* at the Festival so it became a study in prejudice. We studied all different kinds of literature that involved prejudice and then we got into *Romeo and Juliet* which was the perfect play to study. At the end of the year when the kids decorated their writing books that we send home as a gift, the word "Shakespeare" was all over them, but also the word "Prejudice." It depends on the children and the way the year flows.

The kids love to do productions and it's always very exciting, but I think they learn a tremendous amount even if they don't. Some years we've put on small productions in the classroom. There have been years when we've had all the cast from the Festival come see our production. The year we worked on the prejudice aspect, the kids wrote the most incredible things. Here's something that Hannah, one of the students, wrote. "Why is there prejudice in this world? That's what Shakespeare wants us to think about. Prejudice is a terrible thing. Violent words sink into your heart forcing you to say something very mean in return. People use similes and adjectives that are very hurtful. Just because you don't have the same hat or hair or the same color skin. Prejudice hurts." One year we were discussing how old Shakespeare was and the thread of the conversation went to old age and we did a unit on old age. We adopted grandpas and grandmas from across the road. We asked what they thought was old. It was like a river following it own course.

I use Shakespeare as a means to an end. My biggest passion is the writing. When we were studying *The Winter's Tale*, one little girl wrote, "Leontes' eyes were like overheated flames, his cheeks were red as a lobster, grabbing the scroll like child with no manners he screamed 'Lies, Lies.' A hush fell over the crowd. We all wept like wilting flowers. Hermione's brows slid down to her eyes." They write like this. They become the characters. Great writers make us respond as great story tellers and that's what I think is so exciting. The students' understanding becomes so deep. One little guy came in and said, "You know, King Lear and Claudio in *Much Ado*"—we had studied a lot of plays—"and Leontes in *Winter's Tale* all were the same. They believed lies from the people they held most dear." So they achieve amazing things in their understanding. Another little guy wrote, "The world would be less radiant without Shakespeare's plays. They warm the world like a burst of fire." I don't think you have to perform in Shakespearean language to get the children to want to see a Shakespearean play. When they go to see it, they are totally entranced.

In my workshops, I want teachers to know they shouldn't underestimate the capacity of kids. It has to be more than just a performance. Afterwards teachers write me that they never had had that kind of writing before. I know there's lots of controversy about whether you should approach it through the narrative or the language. I don't subscribe to the theory that it has to be either or. It's like phonics or whole language in reading. You use both. I think the more you interact with the story in writing and role playing, the easier it is to understand the words. When I role play with the kids and then go see the play, I understand it so much better because I've interacted with it.

Language takes on a whole new dimension when you study the play. The kids start to be able to predict the meaning because they know the narrative so well. When they're really well prepared, they're just held spellbound by the Shakespearean images that start creeping into the role play.

When we were in Utah to perform at the Utah Shakespeare Festival, at the very end we said goodbye and I stayed on to do workshops and a little girl stayed on, too. She was going to go to Las Vegas with her dad. After everybody left it was kind of like a divorce—it was over—and we felt so empty. I went back to my student housing and there was a little note from her on the door. It said, "Be brave, be not wounded by the great dagger that doth hang in the air. The great chief of knickery did put it there."

When we were going to Utah another little girl wrote in her story, "The old owl went whoooo and the wind doth fly with time in its clutch." And I thought they are really picking up this language.

At one point I talked with the kids about Oberon's speech –

> *Once I sat upon a promontory*
> *And heard a mermaid on a dolphin's back*

Uttering such dulcet and harmonious breath
That the rude sea grew civil at her song
And certain stars shots madly from their spheres,

Well, we were studying that section of the play and I put the words on the board and we talked about them. Then they had to write what they thought those words meant. They had to include the cliff, the ocean, the music, the waves and the shooting star. There was an elective mute in the room who had never spoken in kindergarten nor had he in grade one. In grade two we were doing *A Midsummer Night's Dream* and I am absolutely positive that the writing and the drama helped bring him out of his shell. He'd spoken a few words in grade one, but not very much. At the beginning of the year I had to take him outside to get him to read his work. Then we worked our way into the hall and then into the room. He ended up volunteering to be Oberon and Demetrius and was the Master of Ceremonies at our concert the next year. Here's what he said those words meant, "One peaceful evening I was lying under my secret maple tree on a high cliff listening to the sounds of nature. It was the most beautiful sunset ever. There were reds and oranges, purples and gold. Below me the waves were playing tag chasing the sun in the distant sky. Then I heard music. It was soft at first, but then it grew higher and louder. When I first looked down the waves were pounding against the rocky cliffs. Suddenly they were as calm as a sleeping baby and out of the gloomy sky thousands of stars exploded like fireworks. It was beautiful. I wished I could ride those stars into my dreams."

Here's one by a little girl who fell off a horse and almost died. She'd been in a coma. She wrote, "Surely, the best place in the world, I sat staring over this huge ocean of wonder. The wind blew across my face softer than Christmas pudding, the waves crashed against the rock and tried to swallow my secret for I had heard the most peculiar music. No, it wasn't Bach or Beethoven or Mozart, but wait. It was my music created by me. The music filled the world so completely that the stars became wrapped up. One great star came down to congratulate me."

And then this one, "One girl sat resting on a cliff as high as a cloud. The wind whistled a cheerful tune, the waves below roared like cannonballs. No one knows what Mother Nature looks like, but at that moment I saw her. She reached out and touched my face. Then a breeze caught my spine. It was as if life itself was honoring me for a God. I felt like I was a Queen. The stars granted all my dreams and then snap! Everything was gone. The waves stopped singing, the wind stopped whistling. Life was captured in the palm of my hand. "

When productions are done, this is how Burdett approaches them.

The children usually start off with the life of Shakespeare so he becomes a friend and not someone to be feared. Before they do the play I want them to realize that Shakespeare had children, he had emotions and feelings. The kids pretend they're detectives and they go back over 400 years to see what it was like to live in Elizabethan

England. They write letters and diaries pretending they're Anne Hathaway writing to Shakespeare or pretending they are Shakespeare when the Globe Theatre burns down. So all these emotions and feelings start to come out. They write the last will and testament and birth announcements. Then they are introduced to a play in small sections. They do a little bit and they get really hungry to come back because they think it's very exciting.[iii]

Stephen Haff and the Real People Theatre

Robert Sugarman

The Bushwick section of Brooklyn, New York is *not* Shakespeare friendly. It is a depressed inner city area. But here, too, a gifted teacher created a program that is life enhancing and, given the surroundings, perhaps life *saving* for some of the participants. However, this program is barely acknowledged in its school. Although rehearsals take place after and between regular classes, no performances are held in the school. Haff, a white Yale graduate, who teaches English tells how the program developed with his African-American and Hispanic students in the late 1990's.

The project came out of an exercise in class. When they were studying *Romeo and Juliet*, I had them rewrite scenes in their own words. I said, "Set the play in Bushwick and speak the way you talk to each other." The kids loved doing that. They wrote those and acted them out in class. Those results were so exciting to me that I decided to try and do a production.

In general they're background is working poor. The neighborhood is a ghetto, inner city, and the racial composition of the neighborhood is roughly seventy-five percent Hispanic and twenty-five per cent black. There's a lot of violent crime and drugs. Teen pregnancies. We've had a number of pregnant girls in my classes. Several kids I've worked with have either become pregnant or got girl friends pregnant. The school culture is pretty bleak. There are about 800 entering freshmen each year and each year the graduating class is 60 or 70. The attendance day to day averages about 65 to 70%. Roughly 1500 students are in the school. I think we have the second or third highest dropout rate in New York City.

Originally I had to pursue the kids and say, "You said you wanted to do this. What part do you want to do?" And they'd tell me what part they were most interested in and it worked out and I could just say, "OK, that's your part." Then, once I had the cast the first time around, it was very difficult to get them together. I would call a rehearsal for the whole group and only a few would show up. What I had to do was grab one or two or three people at a time for sometimes just twenty minutes and sit them down and work with them until they started to develop the habit of showing up. But for *Hamlet*, our second production, I called auditions. They all read the "To Be or Not to Be" speech. I didn't base my choices on how good they were as if they were in competition. I would read it and I would talk with them about their understanding of the speech and how they related to it personally. I would have them do it two or three times and see what worked with them and how they took to the process to get some sense of their commitment to it and excitement about it. Based on that I cast them. I also cast kids that I knew pretty well that I thought would have some personal connection to the role. And it was true. In *Romeo and Juliet* and especially in *Hamlet*, they felt that they were the characters. Their ownership of the process brings that about.

Initially we sit around the table—whoever happens to be there—and work on scenes that involve those people. Looking at the script, reading through the scenes. Often I'll read it the first time because it's awkward for them to make sense of it. I'll read it out loud while they follow along. Then I'll ask what it means to them. I don't want them to try to get every single word. I take that pressure off them. I just get the basic intent, the action of the scene. We talk about that. What the characters want and the conflict in the scene. Then we read it again a couple more times and I ask if there's any part they want to change. "Do you want to put it in Spanish or street?"

It's interesting working that way because the first reaction often is to translate everything because they are so insecure with Shakespeare's language. I let them have that room to translate sometimes more than I think should be in the end result. Then they come back. Each time they restored the Shakespeare because they felt it sounded better once they understood it more deeply. They felt it belonged to them just as much as the translation. They did that entirely on their own. It's nice they get to explore it comfortably. In other cases they are adamant about translating sections because they feel the original words aren't expressing their passions adequately. They have an instinct when things have to change to be true to their own voice.

At the beginning I knew just three or four words in Spanish. They taught me a lot so now I know phrases here and there, curses—enough to understand a lot more than I did. But I'm nowhere close to being a Spanish speaker.

Nobody dropped out during rehearsals although a couple times people almost did. They were overwhelmed by other things in their lives, but each time we talked about it and it seemed what they really needed was to talk about their problems. Once they were assured this was a place they could come and be understood, they realized that to give it up would be counterproductive.[iv]

Rafe Esquith and the Hobart Shakespeareans

George Lange

Hobart Elementary School is an inner city school in Los Angeles. Rafe Esquith, who teaches fifth grade, was interviewed just before starting work on the 2003-2004 production of *Hamlet* with the Hobart Shakespearean Company he has created. His school, like Haff's, has many students for whom English is a second language. Esquith wrote of his teaching methods in a book *There Are No Short Cuts* which refers in passing to his work with Shakespeare. In phone interviews, he discussed the Hobart Shakespeareans.

> The first month we learn about Shakespeare and we learn the play. We don't worry about casting at all. The message I'm trying to get across to the children is that is if you're here to be an actor or a star or do something in front of your parents, just leave because that's not what this is about. It's about language and it's about learning to work as a team. The lessons go way beyond what appears on the surface. English actor Ian McKellen is our patron. He's been a special friend and the reason he loves my class so much is that the children aren't actors. They don't want to be actors. They don't have stage parents. He says it's because they've made art a part of their lives. It's like playing baseball. Even if you're not going to be in the major leagues someday, you can play. It's still a great game. So there is nothing wrong with doing Shakespeare or learning to play an instrument if that's not what you're going to do for a living. My experience is that kids who do art are better in everything. That's where I'm at. So we spend the first month just learning the story of Hamlet.
>
> Shakespeare is a terrible read. He didn't mean his plays to be read. The kids have the text in front of them and we listen to the play as we're reading along. Every five or ten seconds—whenever it's necessary—we stop it and I say, "OK, now wait a minute. When the guard says 'You come late upon your watch.' what does that really do?" I break it down

Performing Shakespeare

word for word as to what Shakespeare is really saying. When people watch that process they look at me and say, "This takes a long time." I answer, "Yes, it does. What's your hurry?"

I'm no expert. It took me twenty years to learn this. When kids hear things they understand them better. They memorize very quickly because they actually understand what they're memorizing. Working with children for whom English is not their first language is the reason we do Shakespeare. It helps them with language and vocabulary, with being in front of people. After a month of learning the play, we watch it and with *Hamlet* we're going to watch a lot of different versions. We'll spend two or three weeks looking at Branagh's version, Olivier's version, the Zefferelli version that I call *Hamlet Lite*. I couldn't decide which *Hamlet* the kids should see first—be their first image—but it'll probably be the Branagh because it has every scene. They're going to see all of them. I have the rehearsal with Richard Burton on DVD.

We rehearse an hour a day after school. I do Shakespeare then because it allows kids from other fourth and fifth grade classes to join the project. I think it's important because a lot of time the kids in my class have an "ain't we wonderful" kind of thing going on and after school all kids are welcome. I work with about eighty kids at a time. If kids say, "I don't want to stay after school and do this," that's fine. That's their choice. The other reason I like doing it after school when I would sometimes rather be playing tennis or golf is because it's self-selective. You get the kids who are true believers and since it's my time, if a kid is being a pain, I can say, "You're going home. This is my time now." Whereas if at one o'clock you have a terrible kid, there's not much you can do about it. I think that's a good trade off. I don't spend a second of the hour worrying about discipline, or saying, "Everybody listen up!" Not one second. The entire sixty minutes goes to whatever we're working on that day.[vi]

Kevin Coleman and Mary Hartman and Shakespeare & Company

Shakespeare & Co. in Lenox Massachusetts is a professional theatre that sees teaching as integral to its mission. Kevin Coleman, the Shakespeare & Company Director of Education, discussed the Company's educational programs.

> When the company was founded in '78, we wanted to do performances because we're actors and we wanted to be in schools because that's where kids are learning. Our education program is part of who we are, not something we added on. It's part of the ethic and aesthetic that is set forth in our program. Our

statement of vision states that we wanted "to establish a theatre company which, by its commitment to the creative impulse, is a revolutionary force in society, which connects the truths of the past to the challenges and possibilities of today, which finds its source in the performance of Shakespeare's plays and reaches the widest possible audience through training and education as well as performance."[vii] (See Appendix for the complete statement.) The third part was in the professional training of actors, but now more and more we see that the training actually comes under education

We have programs running all year long. 10 weeks of the Fall Festival for high schools, then we go right into rehearsal for the school tour. Two weeks of rehearsal in December and three weeks of rehearsal in January and the tour goes out during the Spring semester. We use five or seven actors and reach about 100 schools. We go to the schools and do a 90 minute performance or we'll do a venue and kids will get bussed in. We do several matinees at the Founders Theatre here in Lenox, several at community colleges, the Strand Theatre in Boston and the Babson College Theater. A number of fifth grades prepare their version of the production we have toured under the supervision of two directors from our company.

We determine what happens in the schools programs. We learn it again whenever we have the training program that culminates in the Fall Festival. We have two weeks of training for the directors who are actors drawn from the Company. We cover a lot of what they already knew because they have been operating out of it, but they have never seen it really laid out. In the fall for the past 14 years we've sent teams of directors into nine, ten, or eleven high schools. New directors get immersed in the work and returning directors participate in the teaching of it. Then we send out teams of two—an experienced director and a new director.

The design of the Festival is over ten weeks. The first two weeks are the director training. Six days a week, ten hours a day. The second week is director training, but they're also into schools. They run auditions and do outreach into the classrooms so all the kids in the school know about the program. Participants don't have to be in the Drama Club. They never have to have acted before. There's a place for everyone. We need musicians, we need the athletes, we need the kids who are in detention all the time. With the kids who are in detention we've had very high success. Once they do it, they want to do it the rest of the time.

We also do teacher workshops all over the country. We do four day weekend workshops here and in Boston and teachers come from all over. The first thing I do with teachers is try to get them to stop teaching Shakespeare and have the kids start doing it. Over the years we've created a model for doing it, even in a classroom setting. After the workshop, there are 20 valuable things they walk out with. How to deal with the language, how to work on monologues in a classroom setting, how to cut the plays, how to get the students to participate. How to plug into students' multiple intelligences so that every kid can participate. If kids have musical intelligence, they can do this, if they have kinesthetic intelligence, they can do that. The jocks can do the sword fights. They can do the dances. They can create stylized movement pieces. They can do stylized battles in the background. Logical mathematical intelligences can create set designs. Even if we're not going to build a set, we can design it—what the lighting angles need to be. It can include every single kid. If kids are linguistic or love research projects, we give them dramaturgical stuff. When the actors don't know what a word means, it becomes this kid's project of find out who Hippolyta was, who the gods were. Each kid, with whatever ability he or she has, can be included in a meaningful way on the production.[viii]

This limited sample of curricular and extra-curricular Shakespeare programs demonstrates ways to engage students in Shakespeare. Behind each program is committed leadership which is essential to overcome the uncertainties of students. Commitment also helps one deal with opposition or indifference from administrators. Lois Burdett finds support for her work in her school. Shakespeare and Company is brought to schools that pay to have it there. Such support is not always present. Rafe Esquith, as mentioned, had to set up a private foundation to fund his work with the Hobart Shakespeareans after years of doing it out of his salary. Stephen Haff's Real People Theatre does not perform in its own school. The Wooster Group in Manhattan has adopted the Real People Theatre as an adjunct company and Real People raised funds that enabled it to move into its own space in Brooklyn. The positive accounts related here should not diminish how much may have to be overcome to start effective programs. However, when programs do begin—what next?

The Process

The Hamlet School

Lois Burdett starts work with her version of the play. (See Appendix for a list of Ms. Burdett's published scripts.)

> They tell it in my version. For example, with *A Midsummer Night's Dream,* after introducing it with discussion of Shakespeare, they find where the play is going to take place and the kids become Theseus or Queen Hippolyta. They use my text introducing a little bit of story. And then they are asked things like, "How would you feel if you were Hermia and you were forced to marry by your father?" They write and they do a lot of role playing in small sections. Then they write pretending to be that character. Their writing starts to blossom and becomes full of emotion and sensory details. It's often very humorous. They begin to realize they have power with their words. They experiment with language and begin to believe that they're storytellers, too. So it becomes a medium for growth in a lot of different areas. They progress through the play like that. I introduce a section of the play and they become really familiar with the story and then I introduce it with the Shakespearean language.
>
> I think of it the same way I think of teaching a mathematical concept. We begin with the concrete, we move to the pictorial and then we move to the abstract. For example, if I can make an analogy to introducing addition or subtraction, we start there with the concrete—we manipulate base ten blocks. The students do a lot of manipulating. Then we

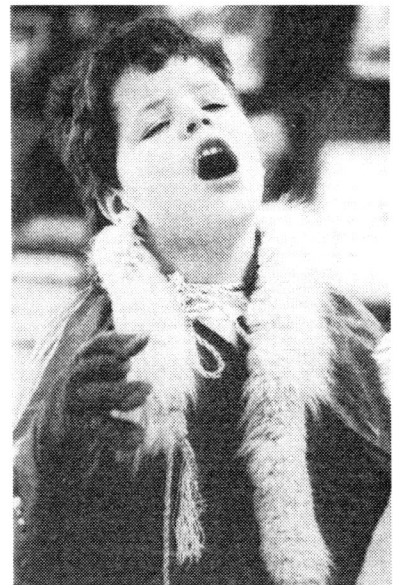

Lois Burdett's Grade 2 students Matt Hunt (Age 7) Sophie Jones (Age 7)

move to the pictorial where we visualize the regrouping concept with graph paper. And then we move to the abstract where they might estimate and solve without paper and pencil. When I think of the two aspects of Shakespeare, I think of the narrative and I think of the language. I don't think of teaching one or the other. I just think of it as one whole just as I don't teach phonics and I don't teach whole language. I use both together to make the student a great reader. When I think about the plays, I think they move through the same stages that they do in math.

For example, the concrete. They start reading my adaptation. The response is quite immediate. The kids like the intrigue and the comedy and the suspense and romance of it all. Because it's only a small portion every day, the children start demonstrating their changing perceptions of characters through their role play and their writing. It makes them really hungry to get to the next part of the narrative. In the concrete we do maps so we find out where the story takes place. Then we have big name tags and sort out the characters and there's role playing. So it's all very concrete.

Then we move to the pictorial. There will be flannel boards and they can move the characters around and flow charts. Then you move to the abstract where you discuss various adaptations and various visual representations and you make comparisons and say, "Oh, look how this person makes Puck and look how this person does."

We do the same thing with the language. We move from the concrete to the pictorial to the abstract. With the concrete we role play various lines—I don't do every line in the play and I don't think it's important that they know everything as they become familiar with the narrative. They start to understand the meaning from the context and all this language starts to appear in their role playing and in their writing quite naturally. There's a lot of Shakespearean language in my books, too. When I use Shakespearean quotes, they are exact. Then we move to where we're acting out various lines and roles and—so this is all the concrete. We might move to the beat of a chant or use music and dances to accompany certain words. I might highlight certain words and they create dances or sing songs. That's all the concrete.

Then we move to the pictorial where they might view a video or a live presentation of professional performers and they start to compare. "Look how the director saw this scene." And we might do a little scene we've just studied. Then we move to the abstract where I take a sample of text and do some shared writing, or shared reading about what this meant to them. We move through all the different stages.

I don't concentrate on performance. What I feel most important is the writing. Then the performance comes. I don't think of the performance or of Shakespeare as an end in itself, but as things that are means to the end. They go far beyond the thought line of a play or even hearing the language. It becomes a tremendously powerful tool to encourage wonderful language and communication. They begin to tap literary talents they never suspected so my concentration is on the writing. I want the kids to believe in themselves and their story telling and to value their own words and to feel the joy of language. The initiative to communicate is in the hands of the children and their words reveal this wealth of knowledge and sensitivity. That's one thing.

I think of all the benefits of doing it with all the areas of the curriculum. For example, in reading, there's a whole new sense of purpose when they begin to find out about the past and what it's like to live in Elizabethan times. They want to know about The Black Plague. How Hamnet died. Things like that. Their desire to learn and the true purpose of reading—all the skills come in. The listening, the speaking, the fabulous comments that come out when they're role playing in their own words. And it's really fun. One time when my Lysander was having a fight with Demetrius, he said "To fight with a jocund jock is madness." So this incredible language starts to appear. That's where my concentration is—in the communication skills, the powers of concentration, their interpretation. When they get into doing a play there are the cooperation skills as they work as a team.

When we were in Utah performing Macbeth, it was fascinating to me and the Director of Education there who said he was absolutely stunned because when they kept moving us from a smaller theater—400 seats—to a larger theater—800 seats—to a larger theater –1000 to 1200 seats, he just stood back and wondered because the kids worked on this almost like a hockey team. They figured, well, if there's a rake on this stage then what are we going to do with tambourines? Where will we put the dolls so they won't roll. It was amazing. When my Macbeth had to be replaced, the Director of Education took over as King Duncan. He said it was an amazing experience because the children led him through it as if they were professionals. With their nuances and their hand gestures they showed him what to do so he just followed the flow. When he was done he went into the aisle and cried for the rest of the performance. There's a lot of cooperation and the end product is a culmination of all these different people working together as a team. That's where the self-confidence comes.

I don't really cast the plays. I never have auditions. Everyday somebody else would be Puck or would be Hermia. "Who wants to be Hermia today? Who wants to be Lysander?" And everyday there'd be somebody different and some of them just suited the part. I had this little girl who had long red hair so when we did *A Child's Portrait of Shakespeare* she was Queen Elizabeth. There was another little girl who was very Puckish and she became Puck. The year we did *A Child's Portrait of Shakespeare* we ended up doing it in a church and the kids walked down the aisle and got married at the front. We had the organ playing and there was a whole congregation of people watching. It was fun. They truly believed they were those characters.

The Real People Theater

Stephen Haff starts with a cut version of the play that he has made.

> I cut the play to what I consider is a manageable size, but then it gets cut further by them in the

Cinthia Candeleria (Cordelia), Marlene Lugo (Kent), and Stephen Haff (Lear) rehearse in a classroom at the Bushwick School in Brooklyn, New York.

process. I cut Hamlet to a little over two hours and then they cut another hour out of it. Mainly they go after redundancy. They'll say, "What do we need to say that for, they already know that." We talk about Shakespeare having done it for a reason. At his time the storytelling conventions were different and the patience of the audience was different so that he could embellish things and have fun with his own virtuosity. He liked to say things three or four different ways. Sometimes they'll enjoy that because it makes sense from the characters' point of view "He's just getting into this now." Or they'll see that that's part of the character's process as he tries to work out his problems. Rewriting the script is their way of making it their own. And they retitled it *Hamlet, Prince of Brooklyn*. They said it's not the same *Hamlet* any more.

At every step they are concerned not just with their individual character, but they're aware of their role as storytellers. They recognize that their character is not in a vacuum and has a function in the story with others. Someone in the audience commented on it—they took collective responsibility for every moment of the play. It wasn't just "You're talking, I'll wait until I talk."

They're not doing my vision of the play. They experiment and I don't tell them, "No." I just ask them questions about their choices. Have them try them out and feel how they work and the things that don't work fall away. The goal is to get this really genuine play where all the choices are theirs.

They are a feisty group and rehearsals aren't always easy. I chose these kids because they are feisty—not happy with the way things are. In rehearsal it's a matter of letting them use that great energy reminding them frequently to put that energy back into the scene. Often they get very passionate about what's going on in rehearsal and they can turn on each other and on me. It's a matter not of telling them "Don't do that," but saying, "How angry you are right now. Use that."

One day a boy came to me upset and said he wanted to drop out. The girl he was totally in love with had cheated on him. Very, very sad. So we started to talk it out and I said to him, "Now go on stage and make that into something. It doesn't have to just sit there in your heart." So he took that sadness and disappointment and made it a part of the character. He was bragging about that just the other day saying how wonderful that was. In general it's making the rehearsal room a place where it's OK to be who they are and express a full range of emotions, but then it's also where they develop strategies for making use of the emotions and managing and refocusing them. Reminding them that emotions are very good—they're very human. It's the choices you make about how to use them.

In *Hamlet* they wrote a scene that doesn't exist of Ophelia and Hamlet being intimate because they felt it was needed. The Ophelia wrote a speech where she tells him, "You can't treat me like this. I'm not your property. I'm a person." And the Queen got to tell off the king.

After noticing how much Haff's students had made the Shakespeare parts their own, the author asked Haff if they could not then go on and do the play totally in Shakespeare's language.

> I bet they could. It's a means towards discovering their ownership of the character and in some cases it created entire new scenes. And it allows them to play with the characters and keep the work alive. They continue to improvise in performance. Maybe 20% of the performance is improvised. They're so good at that. I didn't have to teach them anything about improvising. The one rule was, "Before you improvise on stage, you have to know the play. Then when you have that base, you can play with it." Part of the rehearsal is playing with it. I wanted them to get to a point where they owned it. They had to know it based on what they had created. That conversion they had created. Then they improved again on top of that. So we used improvisation to make discoveries and once the part was learned, to play on top of it.
>
> When we visited Bennington College with *Hamlet*, the kids participated in a class on acting Shakespeare. The project for the day was to take the script and cut it to ten minutes. They read through the play, arranged themselves on stage and then read it again for the other group and it was hilarious. The high school kids were very funny once they got over the awkwardness of the language. A lot of them still look at something in print and recoil. Once they got over that, they were hilarious and their choices were genuine. I think it's important that they don't translate all of the plays into street. That the performance becomes a harmony.

Haff described the background which lead him to his unique way of working with this students.

> I grew up in Canada and came to the States for graduate work at Yale. I got my Masters in Dramaturgy in '92 and moved to New York. I wrote about theatre for various magazines, had a fellowship with *American Theatre* magazine and worked for four years as workshop director at New Dramatists. I also worked for a year as a volunteer with the 52nd St. Project based in Hell's Kitchen doing playwriting and acting with kids in the neighborhood. That's where I got my mentoring and training. I decided the combination of theatre and kids was what I loved most. No more frustration with adult professional actors. So I became an English teacher four years ago.

Asked whether it had been a problem for him being white in a school where the students are black and Hispanic, Haff replied:

> No. It's noticed, but the funny thing is that when we talk about racism in my classes the kids on a number of occasions have asked me if I'm white. And I say, "Well, look at me." And they say, "No, are you white?" It's as if they're getting at some essential cultural thing. And some kids have even said in classes "You don't seem white." It's interesting that their perception is so deep and centered on cultural attitudes and outlook. They are much more sensitive about race and culture than would have been the case in my upbringing.

A student's viewpoint of the work was provided by Cinthia Candeleria who played Cordelia before a *King Lear* rehearsal:

> I wasn't interested in drama. No, not at all. I didn't even think about it until Haff gave a drama class and we started doing certain activities. At first I was quiet because I didn't know what it was I was getting into, but when I started getting up acting and writing dialogue and things like that, I thought, "I like this." Seeing other people's views and what they think about the situations. I wrote him a note telling him I wanted to be in the play and that's when he put me in *Hamlet*. It was originally a guy's part and I changed that. I made it my own. So after that I just made this my home.
>
> It would be hard working with other directors. I'm used to his way of doing it.[ix]

When it was pointed out that she and the others could probably bring their kind of reality to the material whether they changed the language or not, Cinthia said

> It was better for us. We never even did a play before and to jump into it and use some language we don't understand. If we don't know what we're talking about, how are we supposed to act it? It's better working with Haff because he lets us do it the best way we know how. It isn't easy. There's a lot of conflict and misunderstanding, but we work around that and get it done. It makes a better play. If we don't argue before the play, it's not going to go right. It's like a good luck charm. When people are arguing, you can't stop them because that's the way they want to do it. Expressing themselves. It makes a better play because we've let out all that anger and then we can

get the play done. The arguing never stops during the play. Sometimes the arguing makes the person want to leave, but then nobody can work because that person's in the scene and we need them. So why start arguing when you know you have to get it done? But it helps. And everybody's not the same. So everybody's going to argue. People don't like the same things.

Asked about herself, Cinthia replied:

I live with my mother. My father died. That's why we spend so much time together. I have a little sister and a younger brother and we have a baby on the way. My mother is 37 and she looks like my sister. She just holds everything up. Thank God for her.

She wants me to go to college. It's my choice. She does need my help. She's tough, but me helping with the new one coming is necessary. She knows how important college is for my future. She knows how much I want this. She's not going to try to stop me. She's always there. When there's a show, she's there. If she could have come to Bennington, she would have. She came to all of the shows here. Even if she made it late, she still came. She likes what I'm doing. She's proud of it. A lot of parents of the kids in the play don't come. The kids don't have any support, only Haff.

As for colleges, I don't want to rush myself. If I rush myself, I have no clue what I'm doing.

Asked about the role of Cordelia she was then rehearsing, Cinthia said

She's the independent one. She doesn't want to

kiss up to anyone. The other sisters want to use their father. She doesn't want to lie about how much she cares about him just to get a piece of land. She does love him, but he wants her to explain. You can't explain that. Love—it's just there. To explain it for a piece of land? I mean, if you want to give it to me, just give it to me. That's how I'm going to change the part. That's how I am. I'm independent and I want her to be, but you do need people. She needs the father figure, but she doesn't need to suck up to him in order to still be his favorite daughter.

The group went on to rehearse the scene where Lear wakens in Cordelia's presence. Steve as Lear, Cinthia as Cordelia and Marlene Lugo as Kent each had a script and pencils to make changes as they sat around desks that had been pushed together in Haff's classroom. During the rehearsal, Cinthia became unhappy that Cordelia had no response to Lear's final speech.

> **Steve:** (As Lear) *You must bear with me. Pray you now, forget and forgive. I am old and foolish.*
>
> **Cinthia:** *No, you're not.*
>
> **Steve:** You want to add that? "No, you're not!" Or do you want to leave it at that and we walk out together?
>
> **Cinthia:** "I am old and foolish" and I let him think that? (She writes.)
>
> **Steve:** She needs to be strong to make that statement.
>
> **Cinthia:** *I've –*
>
> **Steve:** It's like tough love. "I don't want to hear that out of you."
>
> **Cinthia:** *I've forgiven and forgotten a long time ago.*

Steve: Great! This guy is depressed. He's putting himself down.

Cinthia: *Don't tell me that. And walk with me!*

A transcript of the entire rehearsal is in the Appendix.

The Hobart Shakespeareans

We move from high school students in Brooklyn to fourth and fifth graders who spend a year preparing uncut Shakespearean productions with Rafe Esquith at the Hobart Elementary School in Los Angeles. Esquith described the process.

> There's always the first day where we go over something from the play and I say, "Do you get it? And they all go, "No!" But all the kids who join Shakespeare this year have already seen one or

maybe two or three of the productions and they're dying to be in there. I get more kids than I can handle. They don't understand it at first, but I tell them, "Look, I've done this before. I know kids who have been where you are now. I know I can get you to where we want you to go." So they have confidence in me.

Part of it is because I stay put. Teachers these days last two years and they're out. I'm sorry, no one is that great a teacher in his second year. When I say there are no short cuts, that applies to teachers, too. So many are looking for magic pills. Some teachers get very sad because they come to my room and say, "I can't do that." To which I reply, "I guess you can't because you won't." But they could. Believe me, I'm not that smart a guy. I've never been in a play. I don't know anything. I've never taken a class. I just know that by doing a play every year it encompasses all the skills I am trying to teach the children. My classes are about teamwork. There are classes when you come to rehearsal and it's your turn that day to shut up because it's another kid's time to shine. You're going to have to wait for half an hour and I think that's a good skill to learn—that you're not always the center of attention. That's one of the lessons we learned from Ian McKellen.

The year he met us he brought us to San Diego to see his one man show, *Playing Shakespeare*. Afterwards he said to my class, "How many people were in the play?" And the kids all said, "One, it's a one man show." And he said, "Let me show you something." He brought the kids backstage and said, "Let me introduce you to Mary, she makes tea for me. Here's

Michael who gets my clothes ready for me. Here's John who runs the lights." He showed them there were 35 people. That's one of the things I try to get across to the kids. They are a team. And they function well together.

People are amazed when they come to the show with all the kids onstage, backstage and behind the scenes and there are no adults at all. No one approaches the kids during a two and half or three hour show. My point is that if you need that coaching then I haven't taught you very well.

My wife and I took 47 kids to Oregon to the Shakespeare Festival. There was just the two of us. Usually with a group that size, you have about 10 chaperones. I tell the kids, "If you need that many chaperones, you shouldn't be here." That's where we're coming from. It's about independence and making your own decisions. And my wife has a great question, "What will you do when things go wrong?" Not if, but when because they will. Someone's going to blow a cue, lights are going to go out. Once we had a Titania who fell asleep on stage in her sleeping scene. The kids had to wake her up. But that's OK.

When I cast, I'm looking for a couple of things. The first is can the kids speak clearly. And some kids by nature have clearer voices than others. I know it's wonderful to maybe have some kid with a terrible stutter play Hamlet, but it's not wonderful for the crowd. So I listen to them read and they don't realize this, but I also listen to them speak when we're talking all the time. Who's loud, who's clear. Then I give the kids a sheet that asks what would you like to do?

Do you want to act? Do you want to be on the stage, but not have lines? Do you want to be in the band?

That's a big one because we have a real kickass rock and roll band and we do 10 to 15 songs during the Shakespeare play. Songs that match what's going on. Classic rock and roll songs. We also do classical music. At recess and lunch I teach guitar and music. They are real good. It's not like three chords. These kids can rock. We have about 30 songs for *Hamlet* right now and in the next couple months the kids will learn to sing them all and then decide which ones they want to use. We'll get it down to about 12. We're definitely going to use the Rolling Stones "Painted Black" because that will fit perfectly with Hamlet's mood and his clothes. We use all kinds of stuff from all kinds of genres of music. When we did *The Winter's Tale*, I had three truly gifted musicians—prodigies—and they did the entire Vivaldi "Four Seasons" on violin, viola and piano. They played it all through changes and the play and it was beyond belief. We had a funeral scene for the child early on and we used Eric Clapton's song "Tears in Heaven" and people were sobbing. Plus, when you have sixty or more kids in a play and many of them don't have speaking parts, I don't want to have kids spending all that time holding a spear. By having the band and having kids sing, everybody has something of value to do in the show. The musicians are on stage the whole time. That's something else we got from Ian.

The productions cost about $5,000. We have to rent bleachers so we have raised seating of three or four rows. We can put about 40 people in our classroom. All the kids wear Shakespearean T-shirts that are color coded which clues the audience as to who they are. In *Henry IV* the royal family wore purple. The rebels wore red. Falstaff and his group wore green, but Falstaff wore a wild green. The T-shirts cost like $1,000 a year. We print beautiful programs and then, of course, there are the instruments the kids play. You have to see them. A $6,000. keyboard, state of the art electric guitars, an $8,000 drum set. They're all owned by me and the Hobart Shakespeareans which is a completely separate non-profit corporation.

We're in the school and I go to all staff meetings, but I want nothing to do with the school because they do everything wrong. It's not that the people in my school are bad, it's just that the expectations are so low. It's not even worth trying to have a discussion.

I don't use any speech exercises with the kids because I know nothing about acting. We don't do any acting drills or anything. We just try to understand. McKellen taught us that Shakespeare really is a series of instructions to the actors. What you will do, what you will say. Now how you will do it and how you will say it is up to each actor. My blocking is minimalist. Very few props. Just enough to get across the story, but it's a lot of fun.

As for warm ups, there are two games we play. Bernard Levin wrote this thing that says, "If you cannot understand my argument, and declare it's Greek to me, then you are quoting Shakespeare. If you refer to your salad days, you are quoting Shakespeare. If you act more in sorrow than in anger, you are quoting Shakespeare, " and it goes on for two pages. So the kids do it rapid fire and that's a good way to get them involved. The other thing we do is get the kids to name the 37 plays. When Ian first asked, "Can you name the 37 plays?" my original group at the theatre called out all 37 to the amazement of the crowd.

We warm up a lot musically. That gets the jitters out of the kids and gets them in the mood. It just works. Every year I start a new play and every year I have no idea of what I'm going to do. When we did *Measure for Measure*, we had a nine year old kid play the Duke. It was great. We've done *The Tempest*. We've done *Macbeth* and it really is a bad luck play. We had kids seriously injured in a car accident. We did *Henry V* in front of Peter Hall. That was a lot of fun. We did a hilarious *Comedy of Errors* and we did *Merry Wives of Windsor* so things have always worked for us. We haven't repeated any plays over 19 years.

We perform in the classroom for an audience of 35-40. We do it about 12 times. The 12th show is so

The Hobart Shakespeareans take stage at the Globe Theatre in London.

much different than the first. They've learned so much and they've grown so much. A lot of people know about my class and the guy who does lighting for the rock group Aerosmith designed the lighting for some of our shows. We snuck him in the classroom at midnight and tore out the ceiling. He installed all these lights and dimmer boards and when my administrators saw the place the next day they said, "What's going on here?" I said, "Oh, it just temporary." and they said, "OK" and left. I figure in 20 years the lights are coming down. That's temporary to me.

This allows other kids to work on lighting. The audience is all on one side. We have entrances though doorways and the kids crawl under where the people are sitting to get from one side of the stage to the other. This time we're trying to see if we can get the grave digger to pop up in the middle of the crowd. Henry V did his Crispin Day speech in the midst of the crowd and that was very effective.

We perform mostly for parents and our patrons—people who give us money. There are a lot of important people who are incredibly nice to us. A lot of teachers want to come and see what it's all about. Teachers at Hobart pretty much don't come. I've got used to it. It's something very sad about our society. I always teach the children—this is the first lesson of the year—that there are reasons we do what we do. They range from doing things because you're afraid you'll get in trouble if you don't, doing them for a reward, doing them to please others or out of consideration for others and finally to doing them because that's who you are. That's your code and you don't care what anyone thinks. And that is where we have to get with our theatre. If people come—and they do – from all over the world, that's wonderful. And if people in our own backyard say it's disgusting even though they've never looked at it, well, that's what they think. There's nothing we can do about it. That is a hard lesson for kids who are ten.

One of the reasons it's become easier for me is that I have so many kids who are very successful who come back from college and tell the current kids that doing this is a good thing. "Look where it got me." That's a powerful message. When they talk to the kids it's much more meaningful than when I talk to them. Again there's that staying with it, sticking to it.

There are times when I have to switch actors because I get to know the kids much better as the year goes on. Sometimes it's upsetting. There are always a few kids who don't do what I thought they could. It's not how good they are, it's a question of attitude. And then there are the kids who just grow in the program. For example, our Falstaff. One of the kids last year came from another classroom so I really didn't know him. The other kids in the show were from my class and I saw them everyday. This kid liked to speak so I gave him the part of Glendower and he was hilarious. He was really good and this was around October or November. Then it turned out that my Falstaff had a lot of talent, but no work ethic. Finally I said to him, "Maybe I can get someone to show you that it can be done with the passion I need. So does anyone want to just read the part today?" Timothy said, "I don't need to read it, but I'll do it." He said, "I've memorized it." He started and he was 100 times better than anything I could have hoped for. I asked him how long he'd been working on it. He said, "About two or three hours a night." This happens every year. You open the door and you never know who's going to walk through. I will tell the kids in September, "OK, this is our cast. You play Marcellus and you'll play so and so" and that will change several times over the course of the year. I know sometimes I hurt kid's feelings, but in the real world, there's a reason Kobe Bryant gets the ball at the end of the game. That doesn't mean I like the kid who ends up with the part better or he's a better person, but for this part at this time, he's the one we need. We rehearse about a year. An hour a day. And the play will be in April.

What most people love about my class is the manners of the children. How they treat you and each other. And the parents are great. People's per-

Mentor Ian McKellen with Hobart Shakespeareans in their classroom theatre.

ceptions of parents are curious to me. So many think it's so hard to work with these parents. The parents here are afraid because a lot of them are illegal and the school is official. Every time I travel with the kids, the only questions I get from the parents are I.N.S. questions. They don't understand that if you go to Florida you don't need a passport. They're very afraid of that. I used to take the kids to Europe every year and one of the reasons I've stopped is that there were so many kids I had to leave behind because of immigration problems. In my classroom I have 32 kids this year and I will have one or two parents who are absolutely non-supportive. I have that every year and I have a lot parents who have real issues—alcohol problems, drug problems and the fact of the matter is that even with their problems, I learned that the way you get to the parents is to get to the kids. The kids come home every day excited about school. They work hard at home. They're starting to do things at home their parents could never get them to do before like clean up their room and help with the family. That's how you get the parents. Again, by staying here 20 years, I have a thousand people who want to be in the program—parents talk to each other. There are parents who want to get out of the neighborhood and will wait just to try to get their kids in my class. I have terrific support. Not financial. If I have to keep the kids late—sometimes we're on a roll and the kids will stay with me until 8 or 9 at night and have dinner in the classroom. The parents see no problem. I pay for the dinners. Food is a huge part of our program. The kids are well fed.

The kids here have no problem memorizing large parts. You have to understand that in my classroom there is a culture of hard work and excellence. All day long. It's not like at the 3:00 we say now we're going to work hard to try and do Shakespeare. These kids excel in everything. They play baseball well. We're doing a spectacular art project. We use really good materials. When we played the Beatles' song "Nowhere Man" for Falstaff, the kids sang in three part harmony. The bass player who also played Falstaff and our lead guitarist played it exactly the way the Beatles did. Note for note—an exact transcription. It took them a year to learn how to do it, but they were really playing and that's very important to me.

One of the reasons that I keep the kids for such a long day is that they have nowhere to go after school. I don't think I have the best thing in town, but right now I have the only thing. If they were off to Little League practice—great! But the alternatives here are pretty bad. You can talk about these kids reading Shakespeare because of the way it's presented to them—that's true of most things presented to the kids these days. Like circus training is hard work. It's enormous amounts of discipline and overcoming fear and failing. I love that because that's how you learn.

I'm a 60's California boy. I played a little guitar. Never ever thought I'd be doing music with kids in a classroom. I'm really more of math guy. In the school we have a good orchestra teacher I like very much. Some of the kids meet with her twice a week for twenty minutes and I stupidly thought, "Well, that's their music training. I don't have to do any music." Then in 1991, early in my teaching career, we did *Midsummer* and there is the point where the fairies come out and sing a fairy song. So I said, "OK, let's add a song there. So I added something I liked—a Paul McCartney thing. After the play people came up to me and said, "You're a genius." I thought, really? It was an afterthought. So I was teaching two or three kids guitar one year, then eight kids, now I have 40 kids during lunch and I teach them. I had to teach myself because I wasn't that good. I'm still not that good. The kids are much better than I am.

I do the best I can. I wrote the book and it's got good press and that's helped. I think it's a hit in Canada. I didn't realize what a big issue education is in Canada. People win and lose elections over education. I visited some Canadian cities and the book was wildly popular. *The London Times* ran an excerpt so I'm kind of a hit in England. My wife is a genius. Anything anybody sees in my class that's good, it's probably her idea. Barbara is amazing.

Shakespeare & Company

Kevin Coleman, Shakespeare and Company's Director of Education, discussed some of the rehearsal procedures the group employs.

> You don't have to be able to read to do Shakespeare. We find that the kid who can't read memorizes faster than anyone. That's how he survives in school. When that kid gets up to play Romeo, there's another kid behind him who can read who feeds him a line at a time—flat line read-

Students perform during the Fall Festival at Shakespeare & Company's Founders' Theatre.

ings—no inflection. The Romeo takes it in from hearing it and it's astonishing. The kids in production jump at the chance to feed each other. This stage of rehearsal goes from day one until they're off book. If you walk around the stage with a script in your hand you're limited so we avoid that. From the first rehearsal the Romeo is building a relationship with the girl who's playing Juliet or the boy who's playing Macbeth or the girl who's playing Macbeth—they're building relationships with each other and not with the book.

We show teachers how to work on a monologue in a classroom. Teachers don't want to do Shakespeare because one kid does a monologue while the rest of the class is sleeping. The others aren't included. They're bored. They can't understand what he's saying. So we created an exercise called *It Takes a Classroom to Do a Monologue*. Or a two person scene. Say the scene between Claudius and Hamlet.

"Where is Polonius." "Eating….." The teacher says, "What else do we need in the scene? What else is going on in the story? There's the dead body. We need someone for that. Well, Ophelia can discover her father. Gertrude is sitting alone in her room. The guards on the battlements are moving back and forth because they are about to go to war. Claudius is in the chapel praying. Horatio is worrying about his friend. Laertes is fooling around in Paris not knowing his father's dead." So we have all these realities going on. It takes a whole class to do a monologue.

If you work on Anthony's "Open thy wounds, now do I prophesy a curse shall alight on the limbs of men,"—any time there's a monologue, it's going to be rich in images. Kids think they can't understand Shakespeare because the images come so fast it seems like a foreign language. We're used to eating French fries and Shakespeare writes a 15 course banquet. So, of course, we choke on his words. Our digestive system is not used to that kind of richness.

We work for it to become more personally meaningful to the kids and to the teachers. I always say to directors that over the years we have made all the mistakes it is possible to make and now we're doing variations on some of our original mistakes. We're building a way of work that is more successful, more inclusive for kids with different intelligences. It addresses better the realities that teachers face. We offer exercises that work in classrooms. We've developed ways of thinking about how to work with kids, how teachers can work with kids in classroom settings, preparing them for what's going to happen when we do this work with the kids. When you do

> this work, you meet a wall of resistance and that's where many teachers stop. You have to realize that you are changing the rules on the kids so they'll say, "No, no no!" Then they say, "Oh my God, this is fun." Each year we get more ambitious. New technology comes out so kids are burning their own discs and editing their own sound cues. It's not just actors who are needed to do Shakespeare.

Mary Hartman, Shakespeare & Company's Director of Education Programs, discussed the rehearsal techniques the company has developed for grammar schools.

> The elementary schools work is more structured than our work with high school students. In the high schools we go in and direct plays. There are fundamental differences working in the elementary schools. The students are, of course, much younger and in elementary schools we work during the school day with a regular class of students. We'll work with one class—the whole class—for an hour. We can't do that in high school. It's a developmental issue. By the time students are 14 or 15, they need to be self-selective to do the type of work we do. They don't have the kind of classroom community that an elementary student has which is a more secure environment in which to take risks. Asking high school students to take risks during the school day—scary, scary! But after school they have that kind of community because they choose to be there. They flourish in that context. In the elementary schools we can actually do it during the school day. That's one of the differences.
>
> Then the work that we do is very different. There is a standard model that we've developed—and

there are variations on it, but this is the one we know is rock solid. We do it every year. We use a team of artists—ideally it's three. We work with the class for an hour and the class is whatever size the class is. The artists are actors, but they have to be good teachers, too.

In the elementary schools we lead exercises that engage the energy of 20 or so nine or ten year old children so it requires a lot of performance energy. The attention to the energy in the room is very similar to the attention to the energy in performance. It's really an interesting parallel.

There is a very clear progression in the work. We go in one day a week for 10 or 12 weeks depending on how much money we can pull together for the project and we'll work with each group for an hour. So we'll go in on Friday and if there are four fourth grades we'll work with each for an hour.

At the beginning there's a lot of introductory activity that looks like games. We'll work in a big open space—a multi-purpose room, a theatre, sometimes a cafeteria. It has to be big and open so we can be physical. No chairs! When we sit, we sit on the floor in a circle. We start by introducing the idea of play, the idea of Shakespeare, the play itself, and the idea of acting.

We work towards a specific play which is the one our touring company brings to the school. What's great about that is that it shows them that there is no definitive version because their version with 75 or 80 fourth graders is, of course, going to be very different from the touring production that has six or seven actors.

The first three or four sessions of the ten or 12 are all introductory in which they start to explore the story of the play, the language of the play, the images of the play, the world of the play through physical activities. For example, we have one exercise with a bunch of eight-inch soft rubber children's balls. We create a pattern that they throw and all at once all these balls are flying in all different directions and it's really fun. Then we add words to that, but the words are words from the play. So that suddenly they're hearing all these words and one of the astonishing things I've discovered is how different the words are from different plays. When I go through a play and pull out words that catch my eye, it amazes me how much they conjure the world of the play. I could just read off words from *Macbeth*, words from *Hamlet*, words from *A Midsummer's Night's Dream*, words form *Othello*, and I bet you could guess the play.

I put all these words I've pulled out of the play on little flat slips of paper. They pull the word out of a hat and that's the word they say when they throw the ball. Then it goes backwards so they're throwing the word that they were catching so that the communication goes both ways and they experience the words differently. We started last year to give them more ownership of those words. We gave each kid his or her own word of the week. What was really exciting about this was that during the second week of the project they went to see the touring production. It was Julius Caesar and they came in the next week and said, "Oh, I heard my word!" We hadn't told them to listen for it and they did and got really excited when they heard their words. So that sense of ownership is a real key especially when the language is difficult.

Another exercise involves the images of the play. We'll start with figures of speech and we'll use a bell and say "When I ring this bell, I hate to tell you, but you have ants in your pants." And then they have ants in their pants and we go through a whole series of figures of speech and then we'll get to "You are a dog of the house of Montague." Or "You teach the torches to burn bright." They are moving in space— just walking from one point to another point and then quite quickly we start to give them instructions so that they are suddenly having a physical experience being a dog of the house of Montague or teaching the torches to burn bright or "being a pretty piece of flesh" or being "prince of cats" or having "a pack of blessings light upon your back." These are all images from *Romeo and Juliet*. There's a phrase I use all the time to free them up from the tyranny of being right about it and that is, "whatever that means to you." So if they're not quite sure what a word means, that's OK. They don't have to know what it means. Or if they have a gist of it, but it's not exact, that's OK too. They can go with the gist of it. Another thing that is helpful about it is that kids this age don't edit themselves too much. They give themselves lots of permission. So for the most part the kids are really out there moving and embodying all these things, but those kids who are more advanced than the others and have had that freedom suppressed which happens to all of us as we get older, if they're just walking around the room, that's OK, too. I've often discovered when we come together in the circle at the end and I say, "So, what did you discover? Were there any images that were particularly surprising or that you found very strong?" And this has happened several times—kids who looked like they had just been walking around—what's happening on the inside is just extraordinary and they'll speak about how powerful this image was. Internally they were really having quite an imaginative trip. So the idea behind this exercise is to give the students an experience in an image.

There are two elements in this kind of work. One is the *Text out of Context* so they don't worry about what it's supposed to mean in the context of the play. It just has its own life in that moment. The other is *Literal Meaning*. This is why we start with the figures of speech. To have ants in your pants is obviously a metaphor, but if we let it mean exactly what it says, we get the experience of how that came to be. It's the same way with the images in the text. If we let ourselves be a dog in the house of Montague, that image in its metaphorical sense has more charge over us. The experience of metaphor as literal before we allow it to be a metaphor is powerful.

Another exercise that gives a clear sense of the power of the text out of context is one we call *Text Layout*. You remember basketball layup drills—two people with a basketball run down to the other end of the court. One is dribbling and the other is running and the person with the ball passes it and the person shoots a lay up, scores—there's a high five. That's a layup drill. We often do it first in its basketball context, but with an imaginary basketball. The beauty of the exercise is that it's not just the people who are doing the shooting and the scoring who are involved. All of their teammates are cheering them on and erupting into tremendous cheers when they score that basket. That sets the form for the game. Once they do it with a basketball then we have short lines of text on slips of paper. Instead of a ball, one person has the slip of paper and both people run down—the person without the piece of paper is the actor who faces the audience, the person with the piece of paper is the feeder, stands behind the actor. The actor sees the audience. The audience that is cheering them on stops dead so they can hear what the actor says—so the feeder feeds it and the actor delivers it and scores.

It's exciting to see the different paths people have for their learning. The way people thrive. This *Text Layout* is particularly exciting. Once again it gives the students a chance to have a little piece of text, to have it live in its own world, and it gives them a chance to make it their own with high energy. It's very physical. Everybody's cheering. I've done this with teachers—with grown-ups. Everybody loves it. I think it's because of that high energy and the pleasure of speaking these words. One of the keys is that it's so short—it's easy. Another key is that they're not trying to get it right. Once again, it's the *Text out of Context*. There are some particularly exciting things about this. I'll use *Romeo and Juliet* again, with some obvious ones like "Oh, blessed, blessed night." That's nice and short. "Get thee to bed." Then you start to get ones that when you take them out of context, "You are too hot," are something different. "You are toooo hot" which is fun, but then when it comes back into context with Lord or Lady Capulet who is going ballistic and says "You are too hot." But because they've had that experience of it, it resonates more for them. They get it more when it is in context. With "Thy lips are warm" there is such pleasure when we get to where Juliet says it when she realizes that she has just missed Romeo who has died. It is so much more powerful because we've had that pleasure. So this is one of the underlying principles of the work we do. The words can have all of their meanings.

We've done *Feeding In* with dyslectic actors, but we work with all actors that way. It's also useful in the schools because not all kids are strong readers. Often the kids who aren't strong readers are fabulous actors. They would never get the chance if they had to read while they're acting. Even for me, in my own experience as an actor—and I find it really easy to read, I'm lucky—but it wasn't until I started working at Shakespeare & Company with this approach to hearing the text and being fed that I now never study my lines. I never need to. I just know them. I can't exactly describe what's happening. It's just the aural experience of allowing the text to come in through my ears rather than through my eyes. I just know it and I know it by heart.

Then there are other exercises that are tied to a play. One is called *Character Freezes* where we take ten or twelve lines that a character speaks during the play and several actors will create a group sculpture. Each actor will have one line and we'll suddenly get an experience of Claudius from the beginning of the play to the end. They start to get to know the characters. Then we have exercises in which we do the story of the play with the entire class. These are a little sketchier. We've got three or four different ways of doing this. Because the plays are so different, we don't have it ordered yet into a standard exercise. Usually we do this at the fourth session of the ten or twelve in the elementary schools. In the Middle Schools we have to cut to the chase much sooner. We will go through the story of the play from start to finish with the students participating in the telling of the story using text from the play. We'll feed it to them. A line here and a line there. There are different ways of doing this. I used to have the paperback and I'd say "OK, at the beginning of the play we have Rosalind and Celia—I need a Rosalind, thank you, and this is what's happening and Rosalind says to Celia, bla bla bla and then Celia says to Rosalind, bla bla bla and then so and so comes in." I could barely stand up at the end of the hour, but we'd get through the entire play in the hour. The students would be involved and they would be speaking text.

So those are the goals. It's active. The students participate in the telling of the story using the text. Quite often, if the residency is long enough and in the 10 to 12 sessions it usually is, we do an exercise called *Creating the World* which I love. It's a visual arts exercise. We bring in all kinds of materials—standard art materials—paint, glue and clay and we bring in natural materials. We bring in recycled materials—plastic pieces, just all kinds of found objects. Then we'll have images from the play on slips of paper that the students will choose to create as sculpture—found object sculpture, that is that image. It might be a "tempest dropping fire" from *Julius Caesar* or "disasters in the storm" and they'll build these on little bases that are usually 4x6 mat board. We put them on tiles along with slips of paper with the texts and then put them all on a big table on a board. We'll have 20 or so of these images that are the world of the play on display for the performance. It's a useful exercise because there are some students for whom that is the way in. The tactile, visual arts experience. And once they're in, they're in.[x]

Common Denominators

It should be clear by now that there are many valid approaches to working on Shakespeare with young people. The most important requirement is a strong sense on the part of a director that the work will enhance the lives of the participants. For the director, a background in acting and theatre is useful, but not necessary. Lois Burdett is a second grade teacher who finds the plays vehicles for improving her students' language skills and their ability to work as a team. Stephen Haff brought a background in academic theatre to his work in Bushwick, but the crucial experience for him was teaching acting and playwriting to youngsters in New York City's Hell's Kitchen. Like Rafe Esquith, Haff finds that this work extends the vision of students whose lives are otherwise without distant horizons. Esquith's primary area of expertise is Math. He has no background in theatre and finds guidance in the plays and in his own instincts. His rigorous "There are no shortcuts" approach leads him to spend a year preparing uncut productions. Shakespeare & Company, a professional theatre company, has always seen education as part of its mission. It applies the techniques it has developed for its professional productions to its work with young people.

The groups we have met create environments for the

plays before work on the plays begins. Research into Shakespeare's life, his theatre and Elizabethan England makes the plays more accessible. Burdett shows how active that research can be as she leads her students to explore the processes of simile and metaphor that provide transitions into Shakespeare's rich language.

Work on Shakespeare should not create competition between students with different reading skills. Attention must be paid to the diversity of students and the diversity of their intelligences. The rewards of work on Shakespeare are too great to be limited to "gifted" or advantaged students.

Work on Shakespeare's plays is demanding. The work should also be joyous as youngsters enter his wonderfully imaginative worlds. Each of the four programs we have looked at has found ways to do this.

III: Your Program

Your Program

Approaching the Work

Brian Mason, who has directed in Shakespeare & Company's grammar school and high school programs, contrasted the work he has done at Shakespeare & Company with his own high school experience.

> I wish I had had this in my school because I was taught Shakespeare by a teacher telling us what it was all about. I hated it. I didn't get it. I didn't like it. At Shakespeare & Company we bring Shakespeare to them rather than trying to get them to come to Shakespeare. I think that's very important.[xi]

Mason's experience is not unique. Many of us had Shakespeare shoved at us as something that was good for us, whether we understood it or not. Or it was presented with little understanding that the plays were written to be performed. You should do better.

To begin, choose one play and explore it. Do not try to become a Shakespearean authority—whatever that means, but make that play your own. Read it aloud or with any friends or family you can muster. Perhaps one of the magical plays—*A Midsummer Night's Dream, Tempest* or *A Winter's Tale*. If you can get a modern reproduction of a First Folio or Quarto text, that will help. The First Folio was the first collection of Shakespeare's plays and it was put together by members of his acting company after Shakespeare's death and Quartos were editions of the plays that were published in Shakespeare's lifetime. Although the spelling is irregular there are many clues for the actors in these first texts. The use of capitalization to suggest which words to emphasize and punctuation to show how thoughts hung together were probably composed to convey information to the actors. Starting in the eighteenth century editors started "cleaning up" Shakespeare's plays and this practice has continued to the present day. Although it may make Shakespeare more accessible to the casual reader many tips for performance have been lost. Eventually you will want an annotated version, but do not start with the notes. They can suck the life out of what should be an excellent adventure. Don't stop over words that are unclear. Let the context carry you along.

Next, look at a number of videos of the play and listen to recordings to get a sense of the range of possible production strategies. Of course, if you have access to any stage productions, see them. Where there are disagreements between versions about what happens in the play, make your own decisions. You need no one's permission. Trust yourself with the material just as you will want your actors to trust themselves with it.

Explore Shakespeare's world—its violence, its extravagance—its *newness*. There are many good books and much audio visual material to help you. Michael Wood's 2003 BBC series *In Search of Shakespeare* that appeared in the United States on PBS is useful and the accompanying book[xii] adds fascinating detail. Garry O'Connor's "Popular Life" of Shakespeare[xiii] also has rich material about Shakespeare's world. Remember, that world was physical. London was growing quickly and there was no decent sanitation. People did not bathe as we do. Things smelled. There is a sensory barrier between the Elizabethans and us that the tradition of Victorian and Edwardian Shakespearean production created. In Elizabeth the First's London, heads of convicted felons were impaled on London Bridge as warnings; executions were public and popular. Government spies were everywhere seeking out disloyalty. It was difficult to know whom to trust. The oft-debated question of whether Shakespeare was Protestant or Catholic is not nearly as important as the fact that so much was uncertain at the time.

Making Theatre

Shakespeare wrote plays, something other people have done and continue to do. His may be richer and grander, but the techniques that have emerged for working on other plays can enrich your work on Shakespeare's. The American director Elia Kazan used to say, "A play is an event. Things are different at the end than at the beginning."[xiv] If actors believe in that fictional event, the audience will, too. The director must help actors create that belief. A useful first step is to have actors stretch and relax before rehearsals or performances. Tongue twisters can stretch and relax their voices. Such preparation provides a transition from the outside world to the world of the play.

The conditions of performance make it difficult for an actor to maintain belief in the fiction being enacted. Doors lead nowhere, the lighting is artificial and there is an audience the actor usually pretends is not present. At the same time the actor assumes an identity that is not the actor's own. If the actor acknowledges the presence of the audience as on an Elizabethan stage, one problem is eliminated. Still there is the difficulty of accepting oneself as King Lear or Hamlet. It is also a stretch to believe you are Willy Loman or Roy Cohn in Tony Kushner's *Angels in America*. Techniques for making the fictional reality as great as the reality of performance can help you help your actors.

Through improvisation, discussion or writing, an actor can explore the life of a character within the world of the play before that character steps on stage. Such work should not be academic analysis about the meaning or metaphoric significance of what is happening. It should explore what has happened on a literal level. Such analysis must be done judiciously. If an actor expends too much effort building a backstory, that actor may feel the work is over by the time he or she arrives on stage. There should be enough research to establish the actor's right to inhabit the fiction. Exploring the physical circumstances of a scene—heat, cold, weather, fatigue, etc., can enrich the actor's involvement. The playwright's thought and work is represented by the dialogue of the script. It is up to the director and the actors, working backwards from the words, to create a stage experience that makes those words inevitable.

Many actors find analysis useful, others feel that it impedes them. They prefer to rely on the director to create an environment in which their instincts can operate. It is usually best for the director to understand as much as *possible* and for the actors to understand as much as *necessary* for them to build their performance. Always remember that work on a play is a communal effort between the actors with you, on the sidelines, suggesting that which will help them.

After defining a play's event, it is often useful to break the play into mini-events that fit into the overall event. This permits actors to see themselves as part of actions that begin and end. They can structure their work by finding an overall objective for their role; each moment in the play will have actions consonant with that overall objective. Each action becomes defined as it comes up against obstacles that frustrate the fulfillment of that action.

Some actors are helped when directors advise them to endow elements of the play with personal history by substituting people or places they know or experiences they have had. When the actors mention those things they have referents that enrich their responses to them. The danger, of course, is to develop so much subtext that one forgets the text, but used judiciously, this can enrich the performance. Never underestimate the richness of life experience that your actors—of whatever age and background—bring to their work.

Directing Shakespeare

A director of a play from another time must mediate between the circumstances in which the play was originally presented and a contemporary audience. There is much uncertainty about how Shakespeare's plays were originally done, the kinds of accents that were employed, the speed at which the performances was delivered. The wonderfully imaginative film *Shakespeare in Love,* while filled with wild hypotheses about the events portrayed, does suggest the physical circumstances in which the plays were presented. Costumes, no matter the period of the play, were mostly contemporary castoffs from the company's patrons. The actors performed on a platform with groundlings—people standing on the ground—at their feet. More affluent audience members sat in boxes above the groundlings and above the actors on the stage. A visit to the recreated Globe in London where an all-male company presents Shakespeare's plays approximates the physical circumstances of Elizabethan performance. The reconstructed Globe uses general lighting that illuminates the audience as well as the stage to suggest the daylight in which Shakespeare's plays were performed.

You will probably start by cutting the script to a size appropriate to your situation. Three of the four groups we looked at use cut texts. Rafe Esquith is among the few—amateur or professional—who presents the full text. If editing the text, a director should do so before rehearsals begin knowing that the adaptation will change as work proceeds. Preserve the language in the parts you retain. You may think you will need a narrator to cover what you have omitted, but if you have built your version properly, you will not. Shakespeare's plays accustom audiences to leaps as do contemporary films. Narrations become redundant and the language is jarring

What is the basis for cutting? Steven Haff cites the elimination of redundancies. There is another approach this author learned from Wallace Gray, then a professor at Hunter College in New York. Rather than cut, he advised starting with the most basic elements in the script and adding what is necessary. Romeo marries Juliet and they die. But before Romeo can marry Juliet, the conflict between their families must be established. After their marriage, Romeo refuses to fight Juliet's kinsman and causes the death of Mercutio which forces Romeo into exile. The priest who secretly marries Romeo and Juliet gives her a potion that will enable her to avoid marrying another by appearing to have died until Romeo can return. When Romeo returns, he thinks the drugged Juliet dead and kills himself. She awakens to find what has happened and kills herself. The grieving families begin to reconcile their differences.

This Cliff Notes version is not meant to diminish the play. It is the structure on which a shortened version can be developed. Scenes and characters are added as necessary to develop the script to the desired length. There are other considerations when deciding what to retain and what to drop. Humor based on Elizabethan word play is often hard to make clear. Shakespeare is a bawdy writer and some of the allusions may be inappropriate or misunderstood by grammar school students although in the era of cable television their exposure to adult material is far more extensive than it was for their parents. Classical allusions are often hard to follow. It must be remembered that those directing Shakespeare are negotiating a three way relationship between the play, those performing it and the audience.

Working on a Shakespearean play means you are working on a play that is more than 400 years old. Jan Kott wrote a remarkable book in 1964 that related Shakespeare to an Existential world view.[xv] The truth is that Shakespeare, while firmly rooted in his own time, is always, in Kott's words, "Our Contemporary." After Peter Hall created his rough hewn productions of Shakespeare's *Wars of the Roses* plays for the Royal Shakespeare Company in the 1960's, he wrote

> In human terms the plays are very near to us. I doubt if animal man fundamentally changes at all over the ages. The disciplines and dreams he invents for himself—his religions, ethics, philosophies, moralities—change radically. In these Shakespeare is often far away from us, for our own chaotic public thinking is very contrary to the world order of the Elizabethans. So, what man hopes he is like changes, but not, alas, what he is really like. Shakespeare deals in this constant.[xvi]

But Elizabethans, and especially Shakespeare's Elizabethans, express themselves differently from the way we do. How do directors help young actors handle Shakespeare's language? Rafe Esquith and his students learned from Ian McKellen that Shakespeare offers advice for understanding his plays within the texts. In working on the plays, meanings emerge. Some meanings, however, emerge more slowly than others.

Let us consider some of the ways directors working with adult actors help them understand Shakespeare's language. The Instant Shakespeare Company in New York City corroborates what McKellen says. The company works through the entire Shakespearean canon annually in unrehearsed, book-in-hand performances, guided by the following principles:

1) Unleash the Power of the Words through the Power of the Voice.

2) Speak Shakespeare Swiftly, allowing the words playing off each other to make the arguments, antitheses and word play clear.

3) Don't be afraid of words you don't know. Shakespeare's original audiences didn't know them all either. Speak them with confidence and trust the context to clarify the meaning.

4) Character is revealed through language.

5) Speak, Listen and Learn. When interpretation and ideas can't be played, they are not relevant.

6) Be open to the clues in Shakespeare's original texts. Punctuation, spelling, capitalization and versification in the Folio and Quartos give insights to what's happening with the characters. There were no directions in Shakespeare's theatre and many of these textual anomalies serve as his directions for the actors.[xvii]

The idea of trusting the work to provide the meaning is a useful way to begin. Too much analysis before actors are on their feet can take the life out of any production. The scripts, as transcribed from performance by members of Shakespeare's company in the Quarto and Folio editions, are now available in contemporary typefaces in inexpensive editions.[xviii] However, there will be times when the language remains unclear.

Graham Abbey, a leading actor at the Stratford Festival, grew up in Stratford and has been familiar with the Festival almost all of his life. He tells how Stratford director Brian Bedford urges his actors "to understand every word in the play, to make sure they are clear on what they are thinking in every moment of the play. If you can do that with Moliere or Shakespeare, then the language comes across quite easily to an audience. You know what you're doing. You know what you're thinking. It's tough to do that. It takes a lot of preliminary work."[xix] The meanings actors arrive at may or may not be what Shakespeare intended, but it is crucial that an actor assigns meanings to the words.

English director Trevor Nunn, who has worked extensively with the Royal Shakespeare Company and the Royal National Theatre, goes at it this way. "The only satisfactory approach that I have ever found with a difficult text is to start with the totally naturalistic situation. To work at communicating that situation until language of greater complexity becomes necessary. Until the full text that Shakespeare has provided becomes necessary."[xx] This means taking time to improvise the situation with contemporary language. It is important that such work not be compromised by premature performance deadlines.

Your actors should know that there are many ways to do the plays. Share with them the videos, DVDs and recordings you watched and listened to when you were preparing this venture. When youngsters see the diverse ways the material can be presented, they will be empowered to create their own. Their production will emerge from an interaction between them and the text guided by a director who is sensitive to both.

Engaging the Students

If you teach Shakespeare in an English class, your work can start as it did with Steven Haff by having your students read scenes from a play aloud. When Haff's students were uncomfortable with the language, he had them rewrite the scenes in their own language. This brought them closer to the characters. Once engaged, the language became clearer. Or you might do the *It Takes a Class to Do A Monologue* exercise Kevin Coleman described and involve the whole group in playing all that is going on as a monologue is being done. Rafe Esquith sees the language as a challenge and goes at it slowly with much explication and has his students listen to recordings of the material as they read. Lois Burdett gets her students to create their own figurative language as they start exploring Shakespeare's.

Perhaps you undertook, or will undertake, your Shakespeare program as an afterschool or community activity. In any case, be sure to keep the work informal for as long as you can. If the students are eager for a performance, assure them that a workshop presenting as much work as they have done, is always possible.

Share with the students what you have learned. Remind them of the incredible energy many Elizabethans had. The same people could duel, write verses, dance, and compose music. The night before he was executed, Sir Walter Raleigh wrote a beautiful poem. A painting shows the pleasure Queen Elizabeth took in dancing. Henry VIII composed music.

Remind your students the Elizabethans were like us, but raw and exuberant and, as Shakespeare presented them, amazingly verbal. As England was defining itself as a great nation, its inhabitants were defining themselves as a great people. The Elizabethan Golden Age was brief, but fortunately Shakespeare was there giving voice to its energy, extravagance and fantasy.

Share pictures of the Globe theatre with your actors. Have them do research about it. There is a great deal of material available about the recreated Globe in London. Talk about the intimate relationship of the actors to the audience in such a theatre. You and your students should consider the competitive entertainments that those who attended the Globe visited.

Many young people end up performing on wide proscenium stages that were designed for orchestral concerts. The actors must communicate with audiences across a vast distance. Students in the Shakespeare & Company Fall Festival perform their plays in their schools and then bring them to the thrust stage of the Shakespeare & Company Founders Theatre. For the students this is a significant change. Brian Mason described it for the *Henry V* cast he co-directed in 2003.

> We bussed them in to the Founders Theatre to see *Hamlet* the night before they were to perform. I insisted that they needed to see a Festival show to understand the atmosphere. We had them sit in the front so they could see the audience. In their school there's a twelve foot pit before you can see the audience and here you're standing on them. We kept saying, "Talk to the audience." They realized that in the Founders you can just look out and see somebody and take your monologue right to them. They got it. They totally got it. That helped them a lot.[xxi]

Esquith presents his plays in his classroom. Burdett's productions are so solid in themselves they can be presented in any venue. The best choice is to present productions, if at all possible, in non-proscenium situations. The less production impedimenta, the more the focus can be on the play and on the actors and their interaction with the audience.

Moving towards Performance

Acting is a physical activity. It requires relaxation as well as focus and energy. Stretching and breathing exercises are a good way to start any work—rehearsal, workshop or performance. They also make a useful transition from the busyness of non-Shakespearean life to the life of the plays.

Next, you and your actors need space. Mary Hartman's idea to get rid of chairs is a good way to start. Pat Quigley, director of Education at the Stratford Festival in Ontario, advises teachers and actors working with young people to do the same thing. The rigid geometry of a seating arrangement is antithetical to the spirit of adventure that should accompany any exploration of Shakespeare's plays. When not on your feet, sit on the floor in a circle. Chairs steal energy. This also applies to performance. A standing actor is free to respond and move. A seated actor must first leave the chair and by that time the impulse for action may be gone.

As your actors work on a scene, they must find ways to make the scene's event inevitable. One way is to have them improvise what happens to the characters before the scene begins. In *A Midsummer Night's Dream* Helena and Hermia are friends until the action of the play sets them against each other. They were two girls together, perhaps deciding what they think of the strange Amazon Queen their King is about to wed. "Did you see her clothes?" Maybe they go to Bottom the Weaver for fabric for a garment for the upcoming wedding. Or maybe their families send them to have their bellows repaired by Flute. Anything that will get the actors on their feet and into the world of the play. Remember, the scene is part of a *play*—play with it. Solve what seems unclear by playing through those parts. Intuition based on experience is a match for erudition every time with the proviso that meanings do shift over time and here an annotated script can help.

Be careful not to establish hierarchies among your actors by casting the roles too quickly. Let the actors take turns with them. When you assign roles, do not do it by physical appearance or gender. You may make some wonderful discoveries. Defying audiences' expectations is a way to engage their imagination. Shakespeare & Company's *Feeding In* is an excellent way to keep your actors involved with their partners rather than with a book. The early stage of the work should be exploration and an end in itself. The actors will ask about a production, but hold off scheduling it for as long as you can. If a production emerges, fine, but try to maintain an open-ended approach to the work. Steven Haff's Real People continue to improvise into performance, but only because they are absolutely clear on what is happening at each moment in the play.

The late English director Joan Littlewood led workshops for actors in her productions in the hours before a performance all through a run.[xxii] The workshops included improvisations based on what seemed to her weak in the previous performance. Littlewood's enemy was a performance that had become repetitious and lifeless. Sometimes she had actors exchange roles before that day's performance. "Don't worry about the words," she'd say. "You know what has to be said." Few, if any, other directors have the ability to create an environment that makes such daring possible for actors, but that kind of openness and play within a script is worth maintaining as a goal. So often actors—amateur or professional—want their performances solved before they happen. Littlewood wanted it all to happen on stage. So should you.

Memorization is a problem. At Shakespeare & Company a great deal of memorization takes place through *Feeding In*. Even so, the actors have limited time to work. In the Shakespeare & Company grammar school productions several people play roles so that no one has to master more than about ten lines. Actors pass the roles to one another like runners in a relay race often using a piece of costume as identification for the role. In the high school productions that have seven week of afterschool rehearsals, leading roles are often played by two or three actors. Brian Mason co-directed a production of *Henry V* with two actors, a boy and a girl, playing Henry. Mason felt it necessary that two actors undertake the role. "There are too many lines. One had 220. The other had 200. 200 lines is a lot to give a kid because they still have their own school work. Plus they have to figure out what they're saying."[xxiii]

Rafe Esquith sees it differently. His students take a full year to prepare a production and the leading roles are not divided. "There are no shortcuts!" For Esquith the self-esteem that comes from mastering difficulty is one of the justifications for doing Shakespeare. His fifth graders learn all the lines and have the time to do so.

All directors create environments that affect the success of their work. That ambience results from the director's personality, ideas about the play and relationship with the actors. Directors who don't think about it can establish habits that are not helpful. One famous English director seems to his actors not content "until he has sent one actress weeping to the loo at every rehearsal" as an actress who worked with him told this author.[xxiv]

As you work, be aware that there is an uneven power arrangement between you, an adult, and the actors. The director should make clear that the power will not be used arbitrarily and that the actors and the director are engaged in a mutual undertaking. The director must be willing to listen as well as direct. The director's "what" about the ultimate goals for the work must be flexible enough to adapt to a "how" that fits the actors.

The director should realize that actors are unique and

respond to different sets of cues. The different styles of learning beginning to be appreciated in classrooms are present in the rehearsal room. One kind of direction, one form of notes to the actors, does not fit all. This author had the opportunity to observe Alla Youdina, then the Creative Director New Circus Acts for Ringling Brothers and Barnum & Bailey, train an international group of young performers for an aerial act. When watching three young women working out at a ballet *barre,* Youdina observed

> You see, it's three girls and they do just *foutee* now and each *foutee* is different. Why? Not because of their bodies, because their brain is different and their character is different and I see this character immediately. They do just one foutee and I see why this is good, this is bad. You can write whole story—biography, based on just one *foutee.*[xxv]

To be effective, directors should be that sensitive to the uniqueness of the actors with whom they are working.

It is important that a director establishes safe and consistent working conditions. The rehearsal area should be clean and inviting. Rehearsals should begin on time and end as scheduled. The director should be the first one in the rehearsal space to welcome the actors. A director working with young people must remember that they have things to deal with other than Shakespeare. There are academic and personal priorities they must not ignore. In the author's twenty-five years directing plays in colleges, he never allowed students to use work on a production to be an excuse for shortchanging other responsibilities. Without being intrusive, the director must be sensitive to the complexity of the actors' lives. If an actor is tired, the director must adapt to it. If an actor is stressed, work on a play might be just what the actor needs to forget the sources of that stress. As in the example cited by Stephen Haff, it may be necessary for the director to intervene outside of rehearsal.

Young actors often have a more informal relationship with a director than with other adults because they are involved in creating something together. This means the director may find that he or she hears material other adults are not privy to. While being supportive, the director must not intrude into the actors' space. None of this means abandoning the director's goals for the work. It means recognizing that actors are as much the material that will create a production as is the script.

Moving Ahead

Actors are anxious as they move into unfamiliar territory and should be supported on the journey. A rule this author found useful when directing is to invite actors to ask anything they want about their own performances, but they were not allowed to ask questions or comment about what other actors were doing. Actors can evade their work by criticizing others. A critical attitude can short-circuit creative work. Besides, it is confusing for actors to get direction from more than one source. Directing is a process and a wise director will only say what an actor is ready to hear. Premature criticism, even if correct in terms of ultimate results, can cripple an actor's creative process.

The director must remember that rehearsal not only leads to an end, but shapes that end. A good rehearsal process makes possible a good performance process. Again, the director can not know at the outset how the intended goals will be achieved. This will be discovered in rehearsal. If a director defines intended results too rigidly, the director will limit the actors' ability to do their work. The process of discovery should take place with actors on their feet as much as possible. Seated analysis may be effective until the literal meaning of the material being worked on is understood. Experiential understanding develops as actors face each other and interact. *Feeding In* is a way to develop this.

Directors must remember that a play lives through the actors' performances. If actors have been manipulated into doing things they have not made their own, the play can die. Experienced actors learn to cope with insensitive directors and do the necessary work in spite of such directors when necessary. That is asking too much of inexperienced actors.

As a result of the group's dynamics and experience, the material will be explored on ever deeper levels as rehearsals continue. If the work is aimed at creating a production too quickly, it will be compromised. There is a song in the Kander and Ebb musical *Zorba* about giving things time to develop. In the song, a person opens a chrysalis prematurely and the nearly formed butterfly dies.

Shakespeare's language is so impressive, it is easy to think that speaking it well is enough. It is not. It is still necessary for actors to recreate that which lies under the words. When the actors have not, it is apparent to the audience. Shakespeare performances that are just spoken are hard to understand. The audience gets music, not meaning. When a performance is properly prepared, the audience gets both. This requires a great deal of exploration of the characters' experience and of their language.

Because Shakespeare's plays were originally performed on a bare stage in the daylight, Shakespeare wrote in cues that tell the audience and the actors where they are and what it is like there. In *As You Like It* Duke Senior announces where the scene is set with

> *Now my co-mates and brothers in exile;*
> *Hath not old custom made this life more sweet*
> *Then that of painted pompe?*

Are not these woods
More free from peril than the envious court?

As the scene develops, the actors must create the setting. What does it mean to be in a forest, especially for courtiers unused to roughing it? The nighttime heath in *King Lear* is filled with description of the weather. The elements to which Lear is exposed must be real in the actors' imaginations. In Shakespeare's time, there was probably little more than a thundersheet to create the atmosphere. The actors had to do it.

Rehearsals should not be inadequate performances. They should be part of a process that leads to performance. This is why it is seldom a good idea to have outsiders watch rehearsal. No matter how much visitors are told that they are seeing a process moving towards performance, unless they are very experienced in theatre—and often even then—they will see it as an incomplete performance. Another problem with visitors at rehearsals is that it leads actors to feel an obligation to create a finished performance. Rehearsals or workshops should be unconcerned about the final results until the later rehearsals and even then the exploration should continue while adapting to the requirements of performance. For safety's sake and so that actors will be seen and properly lit, things must be set, but the exploratory work should not stop. Sometimes results will be achieved in rehearsal that the director wants to keep in performance and things can be structured so that an approximation of this will happen. At other times, rehearsals will reveal a process of work that should continue when there are audiences.

Rafe Esquith finds having his casts sing a song from the show is a great way to make individuals into a group that is prepared for work. When this author directed a production of Joan Littlewood's musical *Oh, What a Lovely War!*, he used songs from the show in the same way. Other warm up techniques employ stretching and breathing exercises. Any number of books or videos about basic yoga can provide them and a director need not be an expert to employ them. The great advantage of yoga is its focus on breathing. Deep cleansing breaths at the beginning of a rehearsal focus and relax. There also can be verbal games of the "Peter Piper Picked a Peck of Pickled Peppers" variety to gets mouths limber along with the bodies. And word games are fun.

Preparing for Performance

Decide the physical layout of your production. Set it up so the actors have as direct contact with the audience as possible. Try to avoid a frontal proscenium type situation. Rafe Esquith presents his plays in his classroom with risers for the audience that surround the playing area. A number of performances before a small audience is better than a few before a large audience for many reasons. In a real sense the theatrical experience changes—some say it only begins—when an audience is present. Having moved from professional theatre to academic theatre, this author was always saddened to see months of rehearsal culminate in a few performances. In such a situation, the actors barely have time to adjust to the presence of an audience. Theatre is not about rehearsal. It is about performance. The more young actors can experience performance, the better.

The process of work must not be abandoned once an audience enters the theatre. This requires the director to be in attendance and continue to lead the actors even as they sustain the requirements of a performance. Warm ups must continue. Notes must be given. There must be a sense that the work is continuous. If it ends and the performance becomes a repetition of the previous day's, it is diminished. The director must see that this never happens. If actors move from a familiar performing space to an unfamiliar one if they tour a show, the director must help them adapt to the new space just as the director helped them adapt to a theatre if they had first rehearsed in a different space.

Then there is the question of costumes. At question and answer sessions at the Stratford, Ontario Festival where Shakespeare's plays are set wherever and whenever the directors think will make the play's meaning clear to a contemporary audience, there are often questions about the reason for using such costumes and settings. "Ah," is the usual response, "you want us to wear pumpkin pants. Why should we? Shakespeare's company wore contemporary clothes. Why should we feel bound to approximate his clothes?"

Costumes must be easy to move in. It is terrible when actors' freedom of movement is compromised at the last moment when they are stuck in uncomfortable costumes or in costumes in which they feel self-conscious. Perhaps you think the play would be clearer to audiences if set in a particular place or period. Problems in presenting *The Taming of the Shrew* to a contemporary audience have been dealt with by setting the play in 1950's Italy—in New York's Little Italy in one Stratford, Ontario production—because those locales share the male dominated values that are in the play. Even here, keep the costumes simple and comfortable. Another strategy is to employ costumes from a variety of situations which helps the director and actors create their own timeless setting for a play.

As for sets, the closer you can get to the *platea*, the better off you will be. The theatres on Broadway in New York, once the center of this nation's theatre, are old fashioned proscenium structures in which the audience looks through an imagined fourth wall at a stage picture. In three or four sided theatres, which are closer to the Elizabethan, the expectation of a picture with a setting is minimized if not eliminated. But the Broadway proscenium, like pumpkin pants, still exists in many people's preconceptions of what a theatre should look like. It is also found in the architecture of many school auditoriums. As William Poel discovered early in the twentieth century in England, such settings are antithetical to the speed and direct contact with the audience that is the essence of effective Shakespearean production.

If you must use a proscenium situation, have your backdrop neutral. This will counter the expectation of a literal setting. Shakespeare's language and the acting can create all the setting you need. A few easily moved boxes can do duty as set pieces. Platforms that break up the space can be helpful. They should not have decoration that limits their use. There should be no interruptions for scene changes which take the energy out of a performance.

Lighting should also be simple. You can use general lighting that illuminates both audience and actors. If playing in a three or four sided space, indicate the edges of the playing area with tape on the floor.

Casting is always a challenge. As Shakespeare's company was male with boys playing the women's roles, there are many fewer female roles than male. If you remember that theatre is a game in which audiences pretend to believe that the actors are the characters they are playing, you need not be literal in casting. Interracial and cross gender casting is acceptable to inexperienced, as well as experienced audiences if the actors believe what they are doing. Having said that, this author finds it hard to imagine a Romeo who is not male and a Juliet who is not female or a Richard III who is not male and an Anne who is not female because heterosexual interaction is so important to them. As for many other roles, more latitude is possible.

When do you cast? As suggested earlier, not too soon. If you have limited rehearsal time as do shows that participate in the Shakespeare & Company Fall Festival, you can cast more than one person in a major role. It is fascinating how effective it is when an actor playing a role is replaced by another by handing over a piece of costume or sharing a speech. Theatre is about belief in pretense and such actions engage an audience in what is going on. Again the reminder—audiences want to pretend. Let them. One of the most deadly combinations of sets and costumes this author ever saw was the original Broadway production of *Camelot*. The stage was so cluttered with ostentatious detail, there was no space left for the audience's imagination.

As rehearsals proceed, if an actor is not doing the work, the actor should be replaced. Perhaps, as Rafe Esquith tells the actor under those circumstances, this was not the right time for that actor to assume the responsibility. Such replacements should be rare and only if an actor is not doing the work. The other actors, who are insecure, must not have their faith in what they are doing undermined. But the reality is that once there is a production, the effectiveness of the production must be a priority. The director must make it clear that the decision to replace an actor has been made on the basis of work, not because of personality. When you announce a production, you should announce a time for it to take place. This is why pre-production workshop work which does not have that pressure is so valuable.

The danger is stopping the *process* work of the workshop, as you shape *results* for performance. Actors must continually be given fresh challenges—new actions, new sensory material—improvisatory exploration—to keep the work alive even as things are becoming set for performances. Audiences can be surprising and even hurtful. The director must be there to lend support. Rehearsal is a journey into the unknown and so is each performance.

Many of Shakespeare's plays call for music. There are collections of Elizabethan songs available, but the songs you use can be of any period. Esquith, whose students wear contemporary clothes in performance, uses thematically appropriate rock music. The Stratford Festival did an effective production of *A Midsummer Night's Dream* with a rock score. Elizabethans enjoyed singing and dancing—Shakespeare's company ended performances dancing a jig. Dance and music can employ young people's special skills. In a school situation, it is helpful if it is possible to have music teachers supply expertise you may be lacking. The same with dance. Almost every community has dance teachers. The point is that when a script like *Midsummer* calls for song and dance, the actors must be prepared to do it. Many young musicians can compose.

The same applies to fights. Consult the internet and see if there are any professional fight directors available. Many college theatre programs teach stage combat and may be able to help. If none is available, or if you can not afford such services, battle in slow motion. Even here, choreograph the fights carefully. They are always dangerous. This author directed a college production of *Troilus and Cressida* that required fighting. On the advice of a fight director who was not available to help, the fights were done in slow motion. In the arena theatre where the play was performed, lights came up on a spot, actors rushed into it, fought, and then ran out as the light went out to come up on another fight in another lighted spot.

Do not allow your students to lose themselves in pursuit of a character. Rather, have them find it within. Start with what they have in common with the character, then make adjustments—nearsightedness, an attitude, a vocal adjustment. Sometimes an animal image will help an actor who assumes what it would be like IF he/she were that animal. There have been successful Richard III's based on spiders. Falstaff could be a bear. Again, suggest what seems to engage an actor's imagination. If characterization leads to tension, have the actor start over with a different adjustment

Young people often exaggerate age. A rule of thumb is that as people get older they have less energy. The author once led a successful improvisation with a group of college students who were told to attend their twentieth college reunion. They were advised that in their forties they would not be decrepit, but would be animated by less energy than they now employed. The rehearsal room became quiet. They moved more slowly and were excited to see each other again. All were pleased to discover that a popular couple was still together.

Then there is the question of sexuality. Shakespeare was an earthy writer writing for earthy audiences. Eric Partridge's *Shakespeare's Bawdy*[xxvi] is good guide to many of the references. Because the actors Shakespeare wrote for were all male, there is not a great deal of physical contact between lovers—even in *Romeo and Juliet*. But sexual references and jokes abound. Teenagers can enjoy this word play, but what about plays done with younger children?

Here's how Rafe Esquith handled it with his fifth graders when they were rehearsing *Hamlet*.

> We've watched several versions of the film and that stimulated lots of questions. The way I've explained it is that Hamlet and Ophelia did have a love affair. For them to be that upset with each other, this was not like a first date that didn't work out. And in the Branagh version that I showed them they actually show them rolling around in a bed. My ten year olds know what goes on. They may not know all the gory details and I don't get into the details. What I did tell them is, "The hard part for you guys is when I tell you I want you to be angry in a scene, it's easy for you because you've been angry before. You know what it feels like to be angry. Or to be scared. Or if I want you to laugh in a scene, think of something you once saw that made you crack up. Or if I want you to

feel sad in a scene, you've all felt sadness when a grandparent died or someone you knew was in trouble." I tell them, "It's very hard for you guys to play anything having to do with love, not because it's embarrassing, but be honest guys, you don't know what that kind of love is. You're little kids. So you can't relate back to the time you were once in love." So we watch film and we pretend. That's what acting is. But we're not really in love and that way it relaxes them. Of course when you try and get Hamlet and Ophelia to hug, good luck.

It takes a long time and also we have a classroom where after their first embarrassment, the kids know they're not going to be laughed at by the other kids. The kids respect them because they know what they're trying to do is hard. We do a thing in our plays called a Prequel. When the audience comes in, the room is completely empty. No decorations are up. Then we have an opening song which usually has to do with the theme of the play. During that song the room gets set up in front of the crowd. In *Hamlet* we open with an eleven minute song by Elton John called "Funeral for A Friend/Love Lies Bleeding." It starts with a funeral march and we start with the funeral of King Hamlet. The body is marched in and we see Hamlet grieving with his mother. As he tries to help her off the stage, Claudius takes over. The kids love it and it allows more kids to be involved. At the end of that scene, our band plays and you see the wedding of Claudius and Gertrude. We have photographers take their picture and later on in the play that picture—an enlargement—is on the stage in the background. There's a scene later on when Hamlet is

> very angry in one of his soliloquies and he tears up the picture in front of the crowd. It's fun.
>
> I said if we're going to have a scene of the wedding of Claudius and Gertrude, they have to kiss. When people become man and wife, they don't shake hands. So we do a thing where Claudius—if you can imagine this—puts his hands on each side of Gertrude's face the way sometime when you kiss somebody you touch their face—and as he kisses her he is actually kissing his own hand. From the crowd's point of view, it looks like he's kissing her. The kids actually like it because it's like we're fooling them.[xxvii]

For Shakespeare & Company some of the difficulty is avoided in cutting the plays. Kevin Coleman notes that

> Mostly it comes up when the characters are on some kind of obscene riff like Mercutio and the Nurse. We cut that because it has such a sophisticated understanding of sexuality. The kids aren't even close to that. The kids understand Shakespeare according to where they are developmentally. College kids are at one place—high school kids in different years—middle school—elementary school kids understand it as much as they understand it and that's the level of the story we can tell. In Julius Caesar, the really passionate relationship between Brutus and Cassius is understood by younger kids as friendship. Girls always understand more than the boys do. They have more interest in it. They are more curious about it. Their understanding of it, I would hazard to say, is more sophisticated.
>
> When Shakespeare is taught in schools, kids are

often taught a scholar's or a critic's or a 40 years old intellectual's understanding of Shakespeare. What Granville-Barker said, what that person said. When we work on a play, we present it at the kids' level of understanding of the play rather than an adult's because that's what they can own and speak with personal authority.

It becomes a problem if what you want is young kids presenting an adult's idea of those relationships. The kids can't get that. You can direct them, you can block them, choreograph them into doing things that essentially presents on stage miniature adults. Young kids behaving with sophistication through your manipulation as a director into presenting behavior that they don't understand. Then their acting becomes pretending or realizing a director's understanding of these characters which is much more sophisticated and mature than their understanding of the characters. I think it's abusive to have kids do that. We create performances from where they are at. Their level of understanding. Their level of emotional maturity. Ten years later they'll be able to tell a more sophisticated story. 20 years later they should be able to tell a more sophisticated story, but what is the story they can tell now? What is their Romeo and Juliet now? Or their King Lear now?[xxviii]

The Audience

Audiences project actors into an immediacy that is seldom achieved in rehearsal. The director, who had been a surrogate audience, is replaced by the real thing. Originally the director worked to help actors explore the material. After audiences enter the equation, the director edits the work while encouraging the actors to continue to explore within limited parameters. Actors need notes on their performances. Even the most experienced actors have a limited sense of how their performances are perceived. The author twice stage managed off-Broadway plays during long runs and found it remarkable how wrong experienced actors could be about the effectiveness of their performances. When pushing too hard, actors sometimes came off stage thinking they had been terrific. They had not. Whereas an actor who was not feeling well and only had been able to focus on what was most essential, gave the most effective performance of the run.

Directors have different relationships to shows that have opened. English director Peter Brook sees his work completed when a play opens and believes that there is an inevitable decline after the opening.[xxix] Elia Kazan relied on trusted stage managers to keep his productions alive. Joan Littlewood, as mentioned, believed that the rehearsal process should not end just because a show had opened. American actors Alfred Lunt and Lynne Fontanne gave each other notes until a show closed.

One final consideration. For your productions to exist so that audiences can see them, the productions must be funded. This may mean you will have to go beyond directing and become a passionate advocate in the marketplace. As this is being written, school and community budgets are being savaged and once again the arts are taking heavy hits. The simpler and more focused on acting you keep your productions, the less expensive they will be, but there will always be expenses. Without support from his administration, Rafe Esquith funded the productions in his ghetto school for years out of his pocket. Eventually, he was able to establish a foundation that underwrites the program.

Some parents who are aware of the value of the arts in their children's development and are able to pay for it, pick up the slack when arts funding is not available. Parents who do not have resources to pay for it, can not. Shakespeare did not write his plays for the elite. It dishonors his work to limit Shakespearean production to the children of the affluent. If you are where resources for the arts are hard to come by, you are in an area where young people need the challenge of mastering the wonderful material Shakespeare provides. For children who have many options, Shakespearean production is an additional option. For children who have few options, working on Shakespeare can be a transforming experience in which they learn to work, to cooperate and to achieve.

While the next chapter focuses on creating a single production, the key to artistic and financial success comes from enlarging your vision to a continuing program. To raise funds, it helps to have a track record. It is also important to enlist a support group—a board—that, while respecting the artistic integrity of what you do, works to bring financial stability to your performances. One avenue for a board is to create a not-for-profit producing entity. In preparing this book, the author noted that the quality of work in programs was generally superior to that achieved in individual productions.

Remember what Rafe Esquith said about the value of staying at his school for twenty years? Remember what Kevin Coleman said about what the people at Shakespeare & Co have learned and had to relearn over the years? Even the Instant Shakespeare Company that does unrehearsed performances has developed ways of work over time.

If you are just starting or do occasional productions, do what you can any way you can. Then, work to institutionalize your procedures. It will give you the freedom to develop what you do because you will have a supporting structure and, hopefully, stable funding.

IV:
A Hypothetical Production of *A Midsummer Night's Dream*

A Hypothetical Production of *A Midsummer Night's Dream*

Let us imagine you have decided to work on *A Midsummer Night's Dream*, a magical, romantic comedy with fairies, clowns, two sets of lovers, a King's court and an Amazon Queen. You have read it a number of times—perhaps aloud with others—and have become familiar with different production strategies you have seen in film and perhaps on stage. The more you have seen, the more you have realized that the play offers a director a myriad of choices.

The next step is to develop a set of questions as you reexamine the text. Not answers—questions. Along with the questions, find ideas that the text suggests to explore. The answers and exploration will take place in the later stages of your preparation and in your workshops and rehearsals. This chapter suggests what some of those questions might be and some of the ideas you may want to consider.

Where should the play be set? The script makes clear it takes place in the ancient Greek city of Athens that, in this version, is surrounded by magical woods inhabited by fairies. The Elizabethans had about as much sense of ancient Greece as they did of fairy land so historic accuracy is not the point, but perhaps elements of ancient Greece might enrich a production. Consult books—especially illustrated books—about the art and life of ancient Greece. You will not find much about ancient Greek music, but what about contemporary Greek bazouki music? It probably relates to its ancient origins and it provides infectious rhythms. As for fairies, try to imagine past the Victorian images that are so potent in our culture. Before organized religions took hold, the woods were filled with magical creatures that were invoked to explain the mysteries of the world. Earth spirits. Demons. Mother Nature. Try to get beyond "pretty" as you question what fairies might be like. Think of the mystical woods of fairy tales. Not the Disney versions, but the intense and often bloody versions that preceded them in the tales of the Brothers Grimm and Perrault. Look at Native American, Haitian and African tales. We live in a multicultural world. Feel free to draw from all traditions. Fairies! What a liberating concept!

Then again, the characters *are* Elizabethan. Should you have Elizabethans just saying they are Greek and fairies? Or should you take an ahistoric stance and draw elements from many periods and cultures? Rhythms and images can help you establish a sense of the world you want your production to create. Be curious and explore your options. There are actually four worlds in the play—the court, the young lovers, the workmen and the fairies. Each could have its own rhythm and sound. What might it be?

As in other Shakespearean plays, there is not much question about the overall event. Just as in *King Lear* order is restored, but here we are dealing with a comedy. What does that mean? Tragedy deals with great passions and life and death situations. Comedy deals with everyday, non-heroic situations. The stakes are not as high, but for the characters involved, they are just as important. Think of the great comic actors you have seen—Buster Keaton, Charlie Chaplin, Zero Mostel, Bill Irwin. All undergo their comic ordeals with total belief in their reality. Do not get misled into the idea that work in comedy is less serious than in tragedy. The situations are less profound, but the response to them must be rooted in truth. Those responses may be exaggerated, but only after their reality has been established. Think of Laurel and Hardy walking through a doorway. Who should go first? Who has the key? Where is it? How easily does the door open when the key is found? Will they get caught on the handle? Each physical reality is filled with comic possibilities.

The event of *A Midsummer Night's Dream* is the disruption and restoration of order, but within that are love stories. There are the four young lovers—Hermia and Lysander, Helena and Demetrius; King Theseus and the Amazon Queen Hippolyta; the fairy King Oberon and the Fairy Queen Titania; and the Mechanicals with their love of performance. "Love never did run smooth," so we have a play. All the obstacles help the lovers define their desires and show us who they really are. The whole play *is* like Laurel and Hardy getting through that doorway.

The opening scene is often lost in performance as productions rush to the young lovers. As you explore, take time to explore everything. Shakespeare is filled with riches in lines and scenes that are often cut. King Theseus, a great warrior hero, enters with his intended bride, the Amazon Queen Hippolyta, to ask the court functionary Philostrate to arrange entertainment for their wedding celebration. But what brought Theseus and Hippolyta to this marriage? Theseus says,

> *Hippolyta, I wooed thee with my sword,*
> *And won thy love doing thee injuries:*
> *But I will wed thee in another key,*
> *With pomp, with triumph, and with revelling.*

Theseus defeated Hippolyta in war! What sort of courtship was that? How willing a bride is Hippolyta? By the rules of war, Theseus has won her, but what does she think of this? Only recently they were trying to kill each other. You and your actors must ask questions before you make decisions. How honestly did Theseus win the war? Did he capture Hippolyta personally or did his force overwhelm hers? Was his force larger than hers? Was it an unfair battle? Did the two of them only meet when the battle was over? How resigned is Hippolyta to her fate? Will she try to escape or revenge herself? Remember, one of the basic truths of acting is that characters have not read the play and do not know what comes next. Entertain the alternate possibilities that confront them. How secure is Theseus? Is he rushing the wedding ceremony before something happens that will disrupt it?

There are echoes here of an earlier Shakespearean comedy, *The Taming of the Shrew*—one of Shakespeare's most difficult plays to present to a contemporary audience. In it, Petruchio wins Kate by humiliating her to break her independent spirit. At the end she urges all women to bow to their husband's will. Perhaps in Elizabethan times when women were chattels, this made a kind of sense. Presenting it to an audience today presents problems that are recalled in the opening scene of *Midsummer*. There are ways around the Kate-Petruchio problem. Goldie Semple, a wonderful Kate in a production at Stratford, Ontario explained to the author that she, as Kate, and Colm Feore, the Petruchio, and their director decided that Petruchio and Kate really fell in love and went through all that they did because that was what their society expected. Such a subtext makes the text playable for contemporary actors and audiences, but is it true to the play? Some directors find the dilemma too great and move on to other Shakespeare plays.

It has been noted that your job as director is to mediate between the world in which the script was originally performed and a contemporary audience. This does not mean that you do what was done in the 18th and 19th centuries and rewrite the plays to suit contemporary sensibilities. You do not violate texts by having Cordelia and King Lear or Romeo and Juliet living happily when the plays end. You must be true to the text, but you also must find ways to present it that you, your actors and your audiences will understand. Tragedies must remain tragedies. Certainly there is enough brutality and disaster on the evening news to suggest that terrible things do happen. In Shakespeare's plays they are not accidents like train wrecks or civilian casualties in war. They are explicated in human terms that make them comprehensible. Or, as in the case of *Troilus and Cressida*, the disasters are emblematic of the depths of human folly and degradation.

Act One

In the opening scene of *A Midsummer Night's Dream* there is plenty for you and your actors to explore. Perhaps the mini-event of this small scene is that Theseus wins over Hippolyta. Maybe she sees something in him she had not seen before and permits herself to be won or at least reaches the point where she is willing to consider being won. Perhaps this is the first time she has seen him without his battle clothes. That could mean this is the first time she has really seen him. How can you and your actors find ways to establish and sustain Theseus' and Hippolyta's different ways of being? Perhaps in their movement? His formal and "civilized," hers animal like. Do not underestimate the impact of footwear on movement and character. If Hippolyta is barefoot and Theseus shod in boots it will affect everything they do and in a real sense, who they are. Footwear is so crucial to establishing character, it is wise to have the correct footwear as early as possible. Also, could some sort of accent establish Hippolyta's exotic foreignness?

If, at the beginning of the scene she is a much less willing participant than she is at the end, an event will occur as the scene is played. After their opening exchange, Hippolyta says nothing throughout the scene. This gives her an opportunity to watch Theseus and be won over. Perhaps not. Acting goes on whether or not a character speaks. These are the things you work on in your rehearsals. At the end of the scene, after Theseus has ordered Hermia to marry her father's choice rather than her own, Theseus exits with Hippolyta, but she does not approve of what he has done. He bids her leave with *Come my Hippolyta*, but then looks at her and adds *what cheer, my love?* She does not seem happy with the way he has handled the young lovers.

It may help for your actors to explore the backstory. They can reenact the battle of the Greeks and the Amazons. Doing it in slow motion will make it safe. Perhaps at the end of the battle, Hippolyta is in chains which only come off during the play's opening scene. A production at Shakespeare & Company, started with the battle.

As noted earlier, sensory exploration of the scene—is it hot, is it cold, how are the characters feeling?—can help actors, and through them audiences, establish belief in the scene. In this play where the lovers will wander lost and increasingly exhausted and dirty in the woods, the sensory elements can provide humor that enriches the situation. As in *As You Like It*, genteel folks find themselves for the first time in nature. A production of *Midsummer* at the Stratford Festival had the lovers make each entrance in the woods in costumes that were more ripped and muddied. When the characters have to lie on the ground, it can help to establish that this is the first time they have done so and that the ground is uncomfortable. The more damp, the more bumpy, the more uncomfortable, the better. The greater the sensory reality, the greater the humor. Be wary of having one set of costumes that must not be sullied. It is this author's belief that employing Felix Mendelssohn's *Midsummer Night's Dream* music sets the play in a genteel 19th century world that is antithetical to the play's physicality. Are the fairies going to be fluttery, delicate things out of some 19th century ballet, or magical creatures of the woods? Sensory reality can help create belief in the fiction of which the words are only part.

Hippolyta and Theseus have to go from being adversaries

to people ready—or almost ready—to be married although tensions still exist. Remember that humor and reality do not come from rushing a scene, but from overcoming the obstacles that keep the actors from completing their actions and achieving what they want.

Look at the opening scene again in those terms. Say, and this is only one approach, that Theseus wants to marry Hippolyta because his nation expects it of him. His action is "to marry her for the social good. The country needs a Queen." Say that Hippolyta wants to escape. Perhaps her speech

> *Four days will quickly sleep themselves in night,*
> *Four nights will quickly dream away the time:*
> *And then the moon, like to a silver bow*
> *Now-bent in heaven, shall behold the night*
> *of our solemnities.*

is something she is forced to say as a captive. She does manage to sneak in references to the moon which is, and was to Elizabethan audiences, identified with Diana, the virgin huntress.

There is no correct way to do it, but you and the actors must find your way. Those decisions should be consonant with the play, but often times playing the reverse of what seems to be being said enriches it. Characters do not always mean what they say any more than we do. Social obligations, politeness, interest in some obscure outcome can color what we say. Such an approach gives actors plenty of space in which to maneuver.

Keep the whole group engaged. Just as it takes *A Classroom to do a Monologue*, it takes a cast to explore a scene. In that opening scene, Hippolyta can have Amazon women attending her with whom she will have a more familiar relationship than with Theseus. They were her colleagues in battle; he was the enemy. The court that Theseus is addressing can be large. This leads to an important attitude towards groups and crowds on stage. Joan Littlewood was often complemented on the liveliness and reality of her crowds. When this author asked her about that she had a simple explanation. She had never thought of them as crowds. She thought of them as individuals each of whom was pursuing his or her own actions.

As you explore the scene, have the actors shift roles. The exploration should be about understanding the scene. Hold off casting for as long as you can. One of the hardest things for a director is to know who will, in the course of rehearsal, rise to the occasion. If casting is done prematurely, it is often done on the basis of who is the best reader. It is not unusual to discover that the best reader has demonstrated all that he or she is capable of in the first reading. Remember the success Shakespeare & Company has had with dyslectics who learn their words in rehearsals through *Feeding In*. Shifting the parts will help the entire group share responsibility for the work. Once a way of work is established that is open and exploratory, you and your students are prepared to move into the world of the play.

In French plays it is traditional that a new scene begins whenever a new character enters or a present character leaves. Breaking a play into "French Scenes," each of which has its event, is a useful way to approach a script which is not already divided into scenes. Although Shakespeare created scenes, they can be broken down further. In the first unit of this scene, Theseus announces his forthcoming marriage to Hippolyta and urges Philostrate to prepare appropriate entertainment. What about Philostrate? See the scene from his perspective as anyone playing Philostrate must. He is a court functionary charged with creating entertainment for his king's marriage. This is probably the most important task he ever had. His whole career may depend on how well he does. Often Philostrate, like Polonius in *Hamlet*, is played as a bumbling fool, but each has an important role in the court a fool could not hold.

Now, the lovers. For the humor later in the play to work, Helena must be taller than Hermia. Remember when Rafe Esquith said that a stuttering actor playing Hamlet would not serve the play well? The same is true here. The height difference is not metaphorical, it is a physical reality that is important. We suggested earlier that improvisations creating Helena and Hermia's friendship before the play begins, would be useful. Shakespeare liked the idea of young women as good friends. Here, we only see Hermia and Helena in opposition, but that opposition will be richer if it takes place between friends. It is painful for them to fight. The friendship is an obstacle that can feed the performances of the actors.

In the opening scene Hermia is outspoken in her opposition to her father. What if that does not come easily? What if she has always been a dutiful and loving daughter, but now, like Cordelia, she is beginning her own life which means separating from her father? Would it not be interesting if she is surprised at her outspokenness? She enters as a compliant daughter who may have not seen eye to eye with her father about Demetrius, but when she sees Demetrius and is told with finality what her fate will be if she defies her father, she speaks up. It will give the actress more to work with if she does not enter the scene ready to defy her father. What if her father had not previously suggested how far he would go to have his way? Improvising what happened previously between Egeus and Hermia can help, especially if she does not yet dream of defying him. Whenever the actions and decisions take place in front to the audience, it enables the audience to see more rounded characters. Do not forget Hermia is one of Shakespeare's passionate adolescents. Like Romeo and Juliet, she can erupt into passion and action with no anticipation.

As for Egeus, why is he so adamant? Lysander is as worthy

a suitor as Demetrius. You and your actor must find—probably in improvisation—what makes Egeus so stubborn. Are there frustrations in his life that make him insist on having his way? Is he a single parent who has fallen into the habit of making decisions for his daughter with no wife to moderate his opinions? How successful is he in life that he must lord it so over his daughter? Certainly the society in which he lives gives him the power to do so. It is like the plays of George Bernard Shaw in which men embody the rules of society and women embody a Life Force that defies the rules. It is worth remembering the wonderful final moment in Shaw's massive *Man and Superman* when Jack Tanner, straining to define philosophically what is happening now that he and Ann have agreed to marry, is interrupted by Ann who calmly asks him to "Go on talking". "Talking?" is his exasperated reply? She hasn't been listening to what he has been saying at all. For Shakespeare, as for Shaw, there was a fundamental difference between men and women which developed from the different social spheres in which they live. Men deal with society, women with relationships. For all his competition with Shakespeare, GBS had much in common with the Bard.

Helena is an interesting young woman. Explore the ways in which she differs from Hermia in addition to her height. The more you and the actors can distinguish Helena from Hermia and Demetrius from Lysander, the clearer and more interesting the play will be to your audience. Too often the lovers are presented as an undifferentiated blur. Does Helena respond to things differently than Hermia? She is more verbal and articulates her situation with more insight. Speaking of Demetrius's wandering eye, she says

> *Love looks not with the eyes, but with the mind,*
> *And therefore is wing'd Cupid painted blind.*

At the end of this first scene the plot is underway and the characters established. Theseus and Hippolyta are to be married although Hippolyta's reservations are an obstacle. Philostrate is charged with arranging appropriate entertainment for the wedding. Facing Theseus' and her father's opposition, Hermia is to run away to the woods to elope with Lysander. Helena hopes to win some degree of acceptance from Demetrius, who has spurned her, by telling him of the elopement plans. She, miserable and alone, will defy society and flee to the woods in pursuit of Demetrius. And all of this on Midsummer Eve, the longest day of the year—traditionally the day of erotic intrigue and magic. How can the uniqueness of the date be suggested? Should it be here? Should it be in the woods as the long night begins?

The tone changes in the next scene—the first rehearsal of the play the Mechanicals hope will be selected for presentation at the wedding of Theseus and Hippolyta. To be selected would be a great honor and there would be a significant financial reward for a group of artisans. The Mechanicals, like Dogberry's watch in *Much Ado about Nothing,* lack learning, but are earnest. While their language makes them objects of ridicule, their good heartedness and Shakespeare's compassion for them makes them endearing. It helps to think of the Mechanicals as clowns remembering that clowns were honored in Elizabethan times. Richard Tarlton, a famous clown whom Shakespeare had seen perform, was one of the great stars of the early Elizabethan age. Will Kemp and Robert Armin were clowns in Shakespeare's company. Kemp was probably the first to play Bottom, the Weaver.

What makes a clown? Clowns are intensely physical and each moment is a new experience. Gogo and Didi in *Waiting for Godot* are quintessential clowns who never escape their physical needs. They live in the present. The Mechanicals are separated from the other characters in the play by their social position *and* by the fact that they are clowns. People whose physical needs are cared for, who walk through doors easily, can transcend the physical and engage in abstract activities. Clowns can not. But when secure people are uprooted by war and become refugees toting their belongings on their backs, class distinction and familiar ways of living disappear. The dislocated enter—tragically—the world of clowns. When the four *Midsummer Night's Dream* lovers wander in the forest, they are separated from their comforts and become clownlike, but they can not become real clowns because they are evolving characters. In an internet discussion of clowning, Eric Bagai made the fascinating point that clowns are "unchanged by their experience and remain who they always were."xxx

How can you get your Mechanicals to function like clowns? First, they must think like clowns. Clowns are not stupid. They think continuously and view every object and person and experience they encounter as if they had never encountered them before. Clowns exist in a world of taste, touch and smell. They must walk as if they had just mastered the skill. Circus clowns work to develop defining personas. The German clown Grock was a musically and acrobatically skilled adult with a child's naivete. Everything surprised him. Sitting at the piano in a chair became a battle between him and the chair. When he sat in it, he fell through it. When he finally mastered the chair, he found it too far from the piano. He solved this by moving the piano to the chair. Barry Lubin's Grandma is a feisty elder with surprising skills—she can stand on her head on a whoopee cushion—and has a unique way of moving. She eats her popcorn one kernel at a time, tossing each to catch it with her tongue. Bello Nock is an enthusiastic adolescent with boundless energy and myriad acrobatic skills who takes joy in sharing his achievements with the audience. Giovanni Zoppe (Nino) is also a skilled acrobat, but with the sweetness and rebelliousness of a young child. David Larrible is the endearing uncle who dances rather than walks.

Each of the Mechanicals is distinct. Bottom is a bossy showoff with a sense of wonder. He loves to perform. As the play proceeds, his clown's horizon widens as he enters the fairies' world. Quince, the carpenter, has to be a diplomat to deal with Bottom's enthusiastic ambition to play all the parts. A carpenter's precision might be the key to developing Quince's persona. Snug, the joiner, is "slow of study" which means that he thinks and speaks with great deliberation. Each of these attributes should lead to physical manifestations—the way the characters walk, the way they see and hear. Flute, the bellows mender, is a young man who dreams of being a knight. His emerging adulthood is challenged when he is forced to play a girl, Thisbe. We are not given clues about Tom Snowt except that he is a tinker. Tinkers are traditionally wily outsiders although he seems to have found a home in Athens. Starveling is a tailor. Look for clues to develop personas in the crafts the characters pursue.

Clowns' sensitive responses to stimuli should lead you and your actors to make the scene as sensory as possible. Is it hot? Damp? Is it still daylight? Is one short sighted? Hard of hearing? There is also the tension between a star and the rest of the acting company whom he upsets, but who need him if they are to succeed.

Act Two

Color and tone change as the play moves into the nighttime forest and the world of the fairies. The play here enters midsummer's eve. If lights and sound reinforce the change, fine. They are not necessary. In Shakespeare's time the play was presented in daylight. The tone you and your actors establish should not depend on lighting. There is a useful term in movie making, *Day for Night*, that describes the process of shooting nighttime scenes in full light and then employing processing techniques to create night. The film actors have already created night in full light and so should your actors.

There are two groups of fairies in the play—Queen Titania's and King Oberon's. As romance and sexuality are so important in the play, this might be emphasized by having Oberon's fairies male and Titania's female. If so, and this is only one possibility, when the fairies meet it could be like a mixer between students from an all girl school and an all male school. They know about each other, but except on rare occasions, do not meet and are tantalized and uncomfortable when they do. At any rate, you would be well served to make members of the two groups different.

As the scene begins, one from each group meet for the first time. Titania's Fairy is playful, but dutiful. Oberon's Puck is far more boisterous. Perhaps movement or game improvisations will help your actors establish this contrast. Maybe Fairy's movements are small and precise while Puck's are large and extravagant. How about having the actors improvise a meal with Puck eating grossly while Fairy is fastidious? Some way must be found to help the actors establish belief in themselves as particular kinds of otherworldly creatures. Otherworldly here does not mean from a distant world. Like the gods in Greek mythology, they are exaggerated versions of the everyday. Antennae and spiked heads are not recommended although there have been productions that used both. Have your actors develop distinctive walks. Encourage extravagance as they begin and when they get comfortable with what they are doing, be sure they remain true to their characters. Have each define a spine for his or her character that is real but well beyond the ordinary. Then challenge them to bring in a song or a dance or a movement that represents their character doing what is most true to it. .

It is a while before Fairy realizes that the creature she is talking to is not only from Oberon's camp, but is his most famous fairy. Perhaps your actors might think of it as meeting with a rock star in supermarket. That would certainly be a useful improvisation for them to take for the second part of the scene that begins with Fairy saying"

> *Either I mistake your shape and making quite*
> *Or else you are that shrewd and knavish spirit*
> *Cal'd Robin Goodfellow.*

The rock star celebrity adjustment might prove useful when Puck brags of his achievements. Some productions have two actors play Puck alternating lines like Tweedledum and Tweedledee which reinforces Puck's flamboyance. This also helps later when Puck must move quickly from one place to another.

The confrontation between Oberon, King of the Fairies, and Titania, Queen of the Fairies, presents the traditional Elizabethan roles of men and women—the man expects to be acknowledged the master. It also raises questions about the relationship between people and the natural world for the Fairy King and Queen inhabit both worlds. Titania accuses Oberon of being in love with the mortal Hippolyta; he accuses her of being in love with Theseus. Are Oberon and Titania like Greek gods who have sexual relationships with mortals? Or is it their role to look out for the welfare of mortals whom they love from a distance? You, and your cast, must make decisions about this. The more fully you understand the characters' background, the more fully you will be able to present them in performance. Remember that the strongest possible choices give actors purpose and security on stage. In making choices, there are no correct answers. Shakespeare only gave us what is written. We can find clues in the text, but can not be sure what he had in mind. It is up to you and your actors to fill the blanks.

The battle between Titania and Oberon is so powerful it has distorted the weather and life for mortals. It is like in *Macbeth* or *Hamlet* when discord among royalty—who in the medieval world were perceived as lesser gods—causes graves to open and all kinds of meteorological disasters. Perhaps Titania and Oberon's confrontation explains why there was such discord in the play's opening scene. Often productions of *A Midsummer Night's Dream* present the fairy world and the mortal world as unrelated. How much more exciting it is if there is interaction between them which is what the text indicates.

How do you help contemporary young people portray magic? Do not wait for costumes or lights or makeup to do it. The magic should be developed in rehearsal and be ready to exist on a bare stage in daylight. The popularity of Harry Potter and fantasy movies has made the idea of magic more accessible than it used to be. But how do you help your actors achieve it? Dance movement or circus skills might provide ways of operating that can project your actors beyond the everyday. Have them experiment with different tempos and styles of movement. Explore movement based on different kinds of animals. Do not proceed with the play until you and your company have found ways to create your own kind of magic. When your actors find it, they will have enriched their ability to evoke the world of the play.

Titania and her fairies should function differently from Oberon and his fairies. If Oberon's fairies are male and Titania's female, it will make it easier. Be sure you move beyond stereotypical behavior—jocks and cheerleaders, hoods and their girls, Goths and Valley Girls. Whatever you choose, carry the fairies to the next level of behavior where they become magical.

You must find ways to establish the intensity of the hostility between Titania and Oberon. This provides further reason to eschew the delicate behavior of the kind of fairies who dance to Mendelssohn's music. Shakespeare's spirits embody violence as well as delicacy. There are echoes in the Oberon-Titania confrontation of that which takes place between Kate and Petruchio in *The Taming of the Shrew* except that in the woods there is no social order upholding the man's claim to superiority. Oberon must resort to magic to master Titania. Nothing suggests that he can prevail without it. And Oberon and Titania are estranged lovers. The folio offers a useful hint about their relationship in their meeting. While most editions present Oberon's first line as

> *Ill met by moonlight, proud Titania*

the Folio, which was transcribed from Elizabethan performance, breaks the line

> *Ill met by Moone-light*
> *Proud Titania*

which suggests some forceful response by Titania which leads Oberon to call her "Proud." This indicates a complex and confrontational prior relationship. What keeps them apart here, more than their involvement with adult mortal lovers which would not have been long term relationships, is a mortal child. Often in production the Indian child they fight over gets lost. See if you can find ways to keep him in the action. Maybe even bring him on stage.

After Titania and her fairies leave, Oberon summons Puck. In his lyric evocation

> *Since once I sat upon a promontory*
> *And heard a mermaid on a dolphin's back*
> *Uttering such dulcet and harmonious breath*
> *That the rude sea grew civil at her song*
> *And certain stars shot madly from their spheres*
> *To hear the sea maid's music*

we see that the argumentative Oberon also has the sensibility of a Fairy King. The speech itself is magical. The juice of the flower he sends Puck after will humiliate Titania making her fall in love with the first beast she sees. Oberon's range extends from lyricism to bestiality. What he proposes to do to Titania is not just a joke as it often is presented. It is vicious although it will play out in a comic way. Be wary of settling for a bland and congenial middle course with your Oberon. He is a charmer *and* he is dangerous.

When Demetrius, who is searching for Hermia, enters followed by Helena, Oberon makes himself invisible by saying he has become invisible. If you are working in a space, rather than behind a proscenium, this is a wonderful moment to engage the audience directly in the make believe of your performance. Audiences love to pretend. Let them join in the game of creating a production whenever you can.

Nothing could be less magical than the scene between Demetrius and Helena that Oberon observes. Traditional and well brought up, Helena is so smitten with Demetrius that she has abandoned the female behaviors she has been taught. She violates all social norms by becoming the pursuer. Demetrius, as conventionally brought up as Helena, is the pursued and does not know how to handle the situation.

As the scene takes place at night in the woods, there is real physical danger for Helena. Although Demetrius does not love her, he threatens to take advantage of the situation and rape her. Have your Helena see if she can find moments when she realizes the danger of the situation in which she has placed herself. She wants to be loved. She does not want to be abused. She *says* she is willing to be abused, but does she mean it?

Improvisation in sexual role reversal should help your actors prepare for this scene. Have the girls explore traditional male behaviors. Let them ogle and try to pick up boys. Endow them with greater physical strength than boys. Have the boys experiment with dealing with these advances. Then have pairs enact the scene using their own language.

When Demetrius and Helena leave, Oberon determines to assert his godlike powers by having them reverse roles—Demetrius will be the pursuer and Helena the pursued. You may decide that Oberon does this not to solve their problems, but for his own amusement. After all, he is not a good God like the one in the Bible. He is whimsical like the Greek gods.

When Puck returns with the flower, Oberon launches into another enchanting speech. This one evokes the fairy place where Titania sleeps. Again, the richness of Oberon's language convinces us that he is, indeed, King of the fairies. Incidentally, he urges Puck to carry out his plan to reverse the relationship between Helena and Demetrius. A counterpoint to Oberon's eloquence can be Puck's eagerness to start his errand only to be held back by Oberon's continuing oratory.

For this scene, improvisation between people of greater and lesser status can be helpful. A general orders a response to an attack and the officer who must carry it out tries to get away to start, but can't. A teacher explains all aspects of the instructions for an exam to students who are eager to begin it as the clock ticks. Having the two operate with a different sense of time—leisurely versus urgent, can be useful.

After Oberon and Puck exit, Titania enters in full glory with her fairies and is as eloquent a Queen as Oberon is a King as she urges the fairies to sing her to sleep. This they must do in as rich and sensual a way as possible. Imagine with your actors what the characteristics would be of a fairy bower and develop them through improvisation before you work on the words. Dream or childhood images may help. And there MUST be a song accompanied by appropriate movement. Find or create a melody to go with the richly evocative words. If a distinct style—rock or whatever—has emerged for your production, that should determine the style of the music. Shakespeare's songs are crucial in creating the tone for the events of which they are part. Guy Woolfenden, composer at the Royal Shakespeare Company observes, "The placing of music, time after time is absolutely perfect: songs just have to happen where they do."[xxxi] Just as direct address engages an audience, so does music which audiences perceive differently than spoken speech. Many young people are musicians. Encourage them to help create the music. The worst production is one that does not provide music when the script calls for it. Remember that Shakespeare's actors were skilled dancers and singers.

Oberon sustains the quiet tone as he encounters the sleeping Titania. However, his rhythmic words are an incantation almost as foul as that pronounced by the witches in Macbeth.

While Titania sleeps comfortably, Lysander and Hermia enter the woods exhausted. Their clothing should be totally inappropriate for roughing it. The poetic, musical preparation for sleep of the Fairy Queen is contrasted with their physical state. As many sensory problems as you and the actors can discover—aching feet, pulled muscles—will enrich the scene. Improvisations about camping in inhospitable circumstances can provide useful material.

Lysander's macho certainty that expressed itself in his plan to take Hermia to his dowager aunt's house beyond the reach of Athenian law has collapsed. Like a little boy, he has to admit that he has got them lost. Seeing that Hermia is exhausted, he urges them to rest. Her attempt to make a bed upon the ground has wonderful comic possibilities. She is used to comfort and this is cold, damp, rough ground.

Hermia, unlike Helena, is still governed by the proprieties of her upbringing. She will not let Lysander take advantage of the situation by sleeping next to her until they are married. Don't let your actors rush this scene. It is filled with comic possibilities rooted in the physical realities of uncomfortable terrain and frustrated passion.

When they are asleep, Puck enters. It is worth noting that when Puck discovers Lysander, he acknowledges him in poetry that follows a regular pattern. But when he sees Hermia, he is so impressed by her that the structure of his verse changes. Magical creatures can respond to human beauty. After Puck's exit, Demetrius enters still pursued by Helena who is so exhausted she can no longer keep up the chase when he exits. The physical aspects of her situation must be even worse that Hermia's as she has been running through the woods. It would help if she were wearing totally inappropriate shoes. Her clothes could have been torn in the briers. She is probably sweaty and dirty. Her humiliation at the hands of Demetrius has been enhanced by her beleaguered physical state. She has lost faith in herself by the time she finds Lysander on the ground. When she wakes him, time must be taken to establish the impact of Oberon's magic on Lysander. Explore with your students how to respond to something overwhelming before one speaks. The magic is so powerful that Lysander is shocked by Helena's beauty. When he finds his voice, he declares his love for her. Bedraggled Helena, humiliated by her present state and her bootless pursuit of Demetrius, can only believe that he is making fun of her. Helena runs away and Lysander, pausing only to express his newfound loathing for Hermia, goes in pursuit of Helena.

Hermia has a nightmare that a snake has attacked her heart. When she awakes she finds herself alone, abandoned in the woods. Have your actors explore ideas and fantasies of abandonment. Yes, this is a comedy, but the more real the circumstances, the more comic it will be.

Act Three

When the Mechanicals enter, they are in an unfamiliar environment. Although more accustomed to rough living than Hermia, Helena, Demetrius and Lysander, they, too, are city dwellers unused to the woods. It is night and it is frightening. Besides, they have probably heard tales of magical doings in the woods. Be sure your actors explore these elements as they move into the scene. It may help to have them find their way around the space with their eyes closed or their shoes off which will make them perceive the space differently.

The Mechanicals, reassured by the sound of their voices, want to rehearse, but discover things in their script—drawing a sword, portraying a lion—that might offend the court. Before they can proceed with rehearsal, they have to solve these problems. Similarly, the necessity of creating moonlight and a wall, must be real obstacles that threaten their enterprise. Have your actors take time to explore the problems before arriving at solutions. Just because the next line provides a solution, do not assume the characters know what the next line is until it is spoken. It need not be spoken until there has been a good deal of thought and exploration of alternate possibilities. Puck enters unobserved to watch the rehearsal and leaves determined to fit the Mechanicals into Oberon's plans for Titania.

When Bottom exits and then reenters wearing a donkey's head, the scenic effect must be there. Anything less than a convincing evocation of a donkey's head lessens the fun. Take the time to come up with something that truly "translates"

Bottom's appearance. After Bottom's companions flee, Titania awakes. When she sees Bottom, it is the same as when Lysander awakes to see Helena. The actor playing Titania must convince us that she is seeing the most magical and erotic creature imaginable. As for Bottom, who is the one mortal in the play who enters the fairies' world, he must become as enchanted as Titania. On one level the scene presents Bottom as a bull—or more precisely a donkey—in a china shop. On another, he is a mortal welcomed into a paradise. His braying donkey sounds and donkey behaviors that exaggerate his own Mechanical's behavior contrast with Titania's beauty and delicacy. But while the magic lasts, they are a couple in love.

When Titania first addresses Bottom, he cannot believe she is speaking to him, but her ardor wins him over. Titania's attendant fairies, not having the magical flower's juice dropped in their eyes, may see Bottom for what he is—a man with an ass's head. Or, as faithful acolytes of Titania, they may see what she commands them to see. Try it both ways and see which approach best supports the scene.

After Titania and her fairies lead Bottom to her bower, Oberon enters and then Puck who extravagantly recounts what the audience just saw. Hearing it described lets the audience experience the event a second time. There will probably be a temptation to shorten Puck's speech, but try to retain as much of it as your Puck can keep alive.

Demetrius, who had rejected Helena's advances in the woods because of his love for Hermia, now enters with Hermia who, as in the opening scene, rejects him. In the dark woods where everything seems possible, she fears that Demetrius has murdered Lysander out of jealousy. The greater the reality of Hermia's anxiety, the greater the scene's comic effect. Improvisations about nightmarish anxieties can help your actors. Keep exploring how the inhospitable woods tear at their Athenian gentility as well as their clothes. And there is their increasing exhaustion. After Hermia leaves, Demetrius, discouraged and worn out, falls asleep on the ground. This makes sense if the fatigue of all the characters has been fully established.

Oberon, the Fairy King who can do anything, has, thanks to Puck's error, had his power compromised. He offers no gentle rebuke, but godlike rage. Again, the more passionate your Oberon, the better. Make the stakes high for your actors. Improvise situations in which a person of higher status has plans corrupted by an underling. A manufacturer has his signature product compromised by a lazy employee. In the last minute of the game a coach sends in a foolproof plan with a player who fumbles the ball. Oberon then attempts to rectify things by having Puck bring Helena near Demetrius. Oberon applies the magical juice to Demetrius' sleeping eyes so he will love Helena when he awakes.

Lysander enters with Helena professing his love to her. Demetrius wakes, sees Helena and declares his love for her with the same magic inspired passion that Lysander and Titania had when they awoke with the magical juice in their eyes. As both Lysander and Demetrius profess their love for her, Helena is incapable of believing either. And with good reason. In the opening scene Lysander told us that Demetrius had loved Helena until his affection switched to Hermia. Here your exploration of Helena and Hermia's prior relationship will enrich the scene. They were good friends, but Hermia was the adorable ingenue, Helena the friend who always received less attention until Demetrius courted her. Then he abandoned her. Helena was so devastated by that rejection that she launched into the unladylike actions that brought her and Demetrius to the woods. Have fun developing Helena's history. It will make it easier for your Helena to justify her actions.

When Hermia, exhausted and terrified, enters and goes to Lysander, he rejects her. Her nightmare of the serpent at her heart has come true. Helena assumes that Hermia and the two men are making fun of her. The men argue and soon the women break into one of the most delightful brawls in the canon. Treasure each hostile moment. First Helena is convinced that Hermia is part of a conspiracy with the two men. With a lyric evocation of their past, Helena tries to win Hermia away from the supposed conspiracy. As the tension grows, Helena sees Hermia not just as a member of a conspiracy, but as the leader of it. When Helena starts to leave, Demetrius and Lysander compete in their passionate entreaties for her to stay. At this point Hermia, who still can not believe that Lysander is rejecting her, turns her attention to him. Frustrated by his response, Hermia turns on Helena. Helena responds by taunting Hermia about her stature. The escalating argument should be enriched by all four participants' growing exhaustion and discomfort. As the scene ends the men leave threatening to fight over Helena and Helena, on her long legs, flees Hermia who runs off in pursuit of her.

Oberon's vents his displeasure at Puck. The action here is so clear, no improvisation will be needed to help your actors understand what is happening. Oberon tells Puck to lead the men apart in the darkness where Puck shall taunt each with the voice of the other until they are exhausted and go to sleep. Puck is then instructed to put the flower's liquor in Lysander's eyes so that when he wakes he will again love Hermia. Having been told what will happen, the audience will have the pleasure of seeing it played out. At the same time Oberon will visit Titania. While she is under the influence of the flower's liquor, he will force her to give up the Indian boy. Then he will release her from the magic and, apparently, from all memory of the Indian child. You and your actors must find a way to establish that Titania's memory of the child has been erased. This is an important plot point that is not fully explicated in the text.

After Lysander and Demetrius go to sleep, Helena and Hermia enter and also lie down to sleep. None is aware of the presence of the others. Puck anoints Lysander's eyes and presides over the mortals peaceful sleep.

Act Four

Titania and Bottom are in love. All his uncertainty at her passion is forgotten and he is *translated* from a mechanical to one loved by a queen. While maintaining his luxurious status, the actor playing Bottom must maintain his proletarian and animal qualities. The contrast between what he is, where he is and whom he is in love with, must be sustained. It is like the Christopher Sly interlude in *Taming of the Shrew* where a humble person is able to luxuriate in a position beyond all his dreams. Have fun with your actors exploring parallel situations—waking up in the world of a most desirable celebrity who is in love with you. In the improvisations, rehearsals and performances, probe Bottom's wonder at finding himself in this idyllic situation.

There is another element to be explored. Oberon is watching but has nothing to say until Titania, Bottom and the fairies exit. What is his action before they leave? He wants to see his magic carried out, but would not jealousy at seeing his love throw herself at a mortal with an ass's head enter into it? Might his feelings for her not tempt him to interfere? Or is he taking pleasure in watching her humiliation? Work to make Oberon more than a passive watcher.

Bottom's authority as the Queen of the Fairies' lover is established by his interaction with Peaseblossom, Mustard Seed and Cobweb. Explore their behavior with him. Is it perfunctory? Are they having fun indulging his whims? Do they think he is ridiculous? It depends on what you decided earlier about their attitude towards him. Bottom should be fascinated by each fairy's uniqueness. Since they are given few lines, it is important that you and the actors find ways to make each unique. Explore their occupations for clues. Give them individuated movement. That will be much more interesting for the actors and the audience than settling for generic "fairy" that makes them indistinguishable from each other.

The contrast between the food Titania offers and the donkey food Bottom wants is wonderfully comic if she treats his wants with utter seriousness. Do not let your actors compromise the humor by commenting on it. Titania must remain enchanted with everything Bottom says or does. As they prepare for sleep, wrapped in each other's arms, Shakespeare again evokes majesty through the magnificence of Titania's language.

Oberon summons Puck. He tells Puck how he had earlier encountered Titania in her enchanted state and upbraided her for her affection for Bottom. This provides clues for his attitude as he watched her with Puck. He recounts that when he had encountered Titania, he had her give him the Indian boy and, apparently, lose all memory of the child. His goal achieved, Oberon urges Puck to transform Bottom into his former self with only a dream memory about what befell him. After Oberon wakes Titania, she is appalled to see that she had indeed been "enamored of an ass." The relationship between the King and Queen restored, they and their fairies join in a dance before day comes to end their power. Again, you must find a way to create a dance appropriate to the kind of fairy world you have created.

The fairies and their royalty leave. With daylight, the mortal king, Theseus, and his entourage enter. Theseus and Hippolyta are still very different. He is of the city and the day;

she seems more allied to the woods and the mysteries of the night. However, they now are on better terms than before.

When Egeus discovers the four bedraggled sleeping lovers, he is disturbed that they have been alone in the woods at night. Before he can question their unconventional behavior, Theseus intervenes to suggest the four have come to the woods to celebrate his and Hippolyta's marriage. This seems a good moment for Theseus to show Hippolyta that he is more flexible and understanding of passion than he had previously appeared to be. Loyal courtier that he is, Egeus must accept Theseus' explanation. Hippolyta says nothing as the four explain that now Demetrius and Helena are in love and Hermia and Lysander. Egeus's discomfort at the outcome can balance Hippolyta's pleasure. Theseus and Hippolyta leave, their own relationship strengthened by the happy resolution of the young lovers' problems.

Left alone, the four lovers struggle to comprehend their dreamlike experience. After they exit, Bottom awakens and also tries to understand what occurred in a far more lyric evocation of the differences between dreams and reality. As the only mortal who has entered the world of the fairies, he has to work hardest to come to terms with the experience. His speech is the profound intersection of the urban and fairy worlds of the play.

We return to the world of Athens and of daylight as the Mechanicals discuss their lost opportunity to earn honor and financial rewards by performing for the court. Without Bottom, there is no chance. The interlude before Bottom appears must be filled with the characters' disappointment. Explore with your actors what could evoke such feeling in them. Suppose your production were to be cancelled at the last moment. Then Bottom appears. Not only does he make their performance possible, he suggests to them the mysteries he has encountered although his memory of them is clouded.

Act Five

Hippolyta is fascinated by the account the lovers have given of their adventures. Still, she and Theseus have very different understandings of what has occurred. He dismisses the lovers' tale—likening it to the fiction of madmen, lovers and poets in a beautiful speech that places him as one who recognizes fancies, but has no part in them. Theseus is rational, she is intuitive.

Note the differing ways Theseus and Hippolyta respond to Philostrate's description of the Mechanicals' play. Theseus seems as wise to the ways of the urban world as Hippolyta is to the ways of the natural world. She can not understand his appreciation for the earnest charm of working people. He has sympathy for it and compares it to the tongue tied awe that often greeted him as a hero. Theseus and Hippolyta truly speak different languages. The ways in which you and your actors have defined their differences are crucial for the success of this scene.

Egeus has genuine problems accepting Theseus' decision to hear the Mechanicals' play. After all, his job may be riding on the success of the entertainment. The more investment he has in some of the alternate choices for entertainment, the more he will have to work with. Suppose some of the others are relatives of his who need the job.

The Mechanicals enter and begin one of the great comic scenes in all of Shakespeare. You and your actors must imagine how much this performance means to the Mechanicals. Respect the earnestness and the creativity of their efforts. Acknowledge their genuine determination not to offend their aristocratic audience. It is hard to go overboard in this scene so long as the characters remain true to the personas and relationships among themselves they have established. Remember that comedy should not be rushed. Fast is not funny. Each moment of the scene should be explored for all of its possibilities. Some ultimately will play quickly, others as slowly as you can make them. The dog, the bush, and the wall all present challenges the Mechanicals have solved with earnest ingenuity.

A great challenge for you and your actors is the responses of the courtiers that are, at first, cruel in their condescension. These comments are often lost in the pandemonium of the Mechanicals' actions, but should not be. In the course of the scene, the courtiers are won over by the earnestness and even by the passion of the Mechanicals. Also, the courtiers, as witty sophisticates, are not willing to let the Mechanicals get all the laughs. How much will the Mechanicals be aware of the comments? Will they be hurt or challenged? In fact, the courtiers' witticisms are less funny than what the Mechanicals say and do.

The Mechanicals' dance at the end, like the earlier songs and dances, must be thoroughly prepared. Shall the Mechanicals dance alone or shall the court join in? Everyone participating will create a kind of community that transcends class. If this does not seem appropriate to you, just have the Mechanicals do it. If all participate, it makes a fine contrast for Puck's solo speech that follows. All the fairies enter and have their dance. Then Puck alone offers the epilogue that reminds the audience how much they have been part of the proceedings.

The aim of this chapter has not been to be prescriptive but to suggest an approach to doing a Shakespeare play that will engage you and your actors in a fruitful process. As suggested earlier, this kind of analysis and exploration can be applied to bringing any script to life on stage. If the process is truly explored and adapted to the unique qualities of your actors, you and they will not just put the words of a script on stage, but create the experience that justifies those words. Shakespeare's words are so engaging, one must remember that they are never enough.

Final Thoughts

This book ignored most school, afterschool and social activities because they do not provide opportunities for young people to perform Shakespeare's plays. That is the status quo one confronts when doing this work. If one suggests a program to help young people perform the plays to powers-that-be, the answer is likely to be that the plays are too difficult. This is especially true if the young people fall into a category of racial, ethnic or economic disadvantage. Learn from the people in this book who did not ask permission, but began the work because it seemed worthwhile.

The activities receiving most financial support are those in which athletic elites battle each other. The lesson they teach is simple—to the victor goes the spoils. Team members – isolated by gender—do learn cooperation and hard work, but this book has shown a better way. Those performing Shakespeare's plays are not an elite. Anyone willing can participate. Marginalized young folks often succeed because living outside academic and athletic hierarchies they have not been challenged before. Young people may slouch around in oversize clothes that hide their bodies, but doing Shakespeare's plays they need all of their bodies' vitality to sustain the heightened worlds Shakespeare creates. Participants in Shakespeare programs – boys and girls rehearsing and performing together— also work hard and cooperate as they and their audiences enter beautifully evoked worlds that offer insight into their lives. The plays also teach how rich and dynamic the English language can be and participants learn viscerally the value of art in their lives. Whether they ever do a Shakespeare play again, they know what they are capable of. That is why this book is called *Performing Shakespeare: A Way to Learn*.

Many students—especially the disadvantaged—are warehoused in schools that offer them little opportunity to discover their strengths. The move towards standardized tests has accelerated this. Performing Shakespeare's plays, young people discover how exciting learning can be and how important self-discipline is. These lessons carry over into other work. Performing Shakespeare is a way to make young people central in their own education.

Another force confronting those who would have young people perform Shakespeare's plays is the media that sees young people not as emerging individuals, but as passive consumers of its products. Young people need space in which to discover themselves, to find ways to relate to their peers and to understand those who differ from them. One of the joys of directing Shakespeare's plays is helping students discover their voices as they learn to speak in Shakespeare's.

As well as a pedagogic agenda, this book has a social agenda. At a time when Political Correctness has become a term to denigrate any effort to ameliorate social ills, this book believes that males and females of all backgrounds, inhabiting Shakespeare's magic *platea*, learn that anything is possible. That is revolutionary.

As suggested earlier, it is best to start small. Get passionate about a single play and share your passion with the youngsters. Do not worry about sets. Do not worry about a deadline for a production. Start the work and see where it leads. It will lead nowhere if you do not make the effort again and again against all that confronts you. This includes students who can not imagine themselves capable of doing the work or have not yet learned good work habits. If you are convinced they can do it, they probably can.

As you work, be supportive of your actors—all actors are vulnerable—but be critical of what you do. Have you explored all the possibilities of the material? Have you helped each actor go as far as possible? Performing Shakespeare's plays is not enough. It must be done in ways that are meaningful to the participants and enrich the audience's understanding of the plays.

This book looked at programs—not individual productions. A program is a series of productions that permits directors to develop their own ways to engage youngsters with the material. The plays are so various, you and the young people you work with will want to continue to explore them once you have started. A single production can be exciting; a program provides you and your actors opportunities to inhabit a variety of contexts and, as Mary Hartman noted, each play has unique language you and your actors will want to explore.. When work on Shakespeare's plays is ongoing, it develops its own traditions about ways to do the material even as it adapts to the demands of different plays. Audiences, too, will learn to welcome the work as it becomes expected. The burden of "doing Shakespeare" is diminished when it is a continuing process Over time administrators may even understand the value of what you are doing.

Never forget that people have had a wonderful time bringing Shakespeare's plays to life for over four hundred years in many different situations. Good luck as you participate in the community that has shared the wonder of Shakespeare's plays.

Caitlin Ellison (age 8), student of Lois Burdett

Appendix

Further Information about the Groups Discussed

Lois Burdett

Ms. Burdett's books in the *Shakespeare Can Be Fun* Series published by Firefly Books are
Much Ado About Nothing for Kids by Lois Burdett, foreword by Denzel Washington.
    ISBN: 1-55209-413-8 paperback
    ISBN: 1-55209-411-1 library binding
Hamlet for Kids by Lois Burdett, introduction by Kenneth Branagh
    ISBN: 1-55209-530-4 paperback
    ISBN: 1-55209-522-3 library binding
The Tempest for Kids by Lois Burdett
    ISBN: 1-55209-326-3 paperback
    ISBN: 1-55209-355-7 library binding
Romeo and Juliet for Kids by Lois Burdett
    ISBN: 1-55209-229-1 paperback
    ISBN: 1-55209-244-5 library binding
A Midsummer Night's Dream for Kids by Lois Burdett
    ISBN: 1-55209-124-4 paperback
    ISBN: 1-55209-130-9 library binding
Macbeth for Kids by Lois Burdett
    ISBN: 0-88753-279-9 paperback
    ISBN: 0-88753-287-X library binding
A Child's Portrait of Shakespeare by Lois Burdett
    ISBN: 088753-261-6 paperback
    ISBN: 088753-263-2 library binding

Twelfth Night for Kids by Lois Burdett and Christine Coburn
ISBN: 088753-233-0 paperback.

All the books are available from Firefly Books
http://www.Fireflybooks.com/kids/Shakespeare.html

An excellent 48 minute documentary video of Ms. Burdett doing Shakespeare with children, *The Secret of Will*, is available from Twilight Films, 526 Palmerston Blvd., Suite C, Toronto, Ontario Canada M6G 2P5.
e-mail: **downeast@wiznet.ca** Toll free: 1-800-268-2495.

Ms. Burdett conducts teacher workshops and can be contacted at e-mail: **lburdett@Shakespearecanbefun.com**

Cinthia Candeleria,

Marlene Lugo, Real People Theater

Robert Sugarman

Real People Theater

The company's official biography

The Real People Theater Company, Inc.
Real People Theater (RPT) is a company of young actors who met at Bushwick High School in Brooklyn. They rework classic and modern plays into what they call the Ghetto Remix, a combination of the original words, Spanish and Street. RPT has taken *Romeo y Julieta*, *Hamlet Prince of Brooklyn*, *King Lear: Brooklyn Remix* and Canadian star George Walker's *Tough* to colleges all over NYC, including Brooklyn College, NYU, The New School, and to Bennington College in Vermont. This Thanksgiving, *Tough* visited Nova Scotia. As a direct result of these trips, two former Latin King gang members are now enrolled as students at Bennington College and all graduating RPT actors have gone on to higher education. Fordham University at Lincoln Center created a course in its curriculum for collaboration between their theater students and RPT, which has resulted in shared productions of *Waiting for Lefty*, by Clifford Odets, and Brecht's *The Exception and the Rule*. RPT has also performed to great acclaim at professional theaters in NYC such as The Flea, New Dramatists, Repertorio Espanol, The Collapsible Hole, The Nest and The Performing Garage. The world-famous Wooster Group has adopted RPT as its official apprentice company. Beyond New York, in addition to the three-year relationship with Bennington, RPT has taken its work to theaters, high schools and colleges in Los Angeles, Chicago and Toronto, where Walker said he has been trying for 30 years to get professional actors to do what these kids are

doing. This past summer RPT traveled to Germany with its first commission, *Ring Around the Royalty, the Remix of the Ancient Nibelungenlied*. While RPT's work is open to a general audience, its primary mission is to reach teens. At present, RPT serves some 30 Bushwick students and affects hundreds more in the audiences for each project. After every performance, the actors run a discussion with the audience. Teens have sworn that these shows and conversations have taught them more about making important choices than any classroom ever has. Real People Theater has been profiled in The Village Voice, Urban Latino, The Brooklyn Rail, The Word on the Street, The Waterloo Chronicle, Theater2K, Mannheimer Morgen, Go Brooklyn, Education Notes and The Chicago Reader, who said of the actors in *Tough*, "The performances deliver enough soul, guts and heart to teach older actors a thing or three."

This season, thanks to a generous gift from the Annenberg Foundation, RPT opens its new home in the Bushwick neighborhood. The season includes the revival of *King Lear*, *Tough* and *Ring Around the Royalty*, along with the new project, *Paradise Lost*. (2004)

The Company can be contacted at
realpeopletheatercompany@hotmail.com

Transcript of a Real People Theater *King Lear* Rehearsal

Steven Haff plays Lear, Cinthia Candeleria plays Cordelia, Marlene Lugo plays Kent. The printed program attributes direction to Candeleria, Haff, Doris Santiago and Albert Young.

Steve: The doctor is not here. He's a bilingual student—hardly speaks any English. He's going to do his lines in Spanish. Marlene, your idea is that you are going to translate what he says so that Cordelia can understand. When Cinthia feels it's appropriate, she's going to carry on her own conversation in Spanish.

Cinthia: I understand Spanish, but I don't know how to speak it. So maybe she should translate what I say.

Steve: OK. Marlene, you translate for her to him. So let's read this. This is during the war and I, the King, have finally met up with Cordelia, my daughter.

Cinthia: *Oh thou Good Kent. How shall I live and work*
To match thy goodness? My life will be too short
And every measure fail me.

Steve: What are you saying? "How shall I live and work to match thy goodness?"

Cinthia: Whose goodness? Hers?

Steve: Yes.

Cinthia: What can I do to do what she's doing?

Steve: Yes. To be as good as she is. Because she has stuck by me through all of this and you're saying—

Cinthia: "*Damn Kent, how shall I live and work*
To match your goodness? My life will be too short.
And every measure has been - -

Steve: You're saying my life will be too short and every measure will fail me.

Cinthia: So every measure WILL fail me.

Marlene: *To be acknowledged, madam, is overpaid.*

Steve: She's saying, "What can I possible do to thank you for this, to come up to your level to show my appreciation" and you're saying, "To be acknowledged, madam, is overpaid."

Cinthia: The recognition is enough.

Steve: Yes. Acknowledgment is to be overpaid. Why don't you add in "to be." "To be acknowledged madam, is <u>to be</u> overpaid." Read on.

Marlene: *All my reports go with the modest truth.*
Nor more nor clipped, but so.

Steve: So what do you think you're saying there?

Cinthia: Everything you did was real and true.

Steve: Yes. So, what matters to me is the truth. Nothing more, nothing less. How do you want to put that?

Marlene: *To be acknowledged, Cordelia - -*

Steve: She doesn't want to say "Madam."

Cinthia: I am "Madam."

Steve: She'd rather not address you that way so it'll be clearer.

The next two lines, Marlene?

Marlene*: All my reports go with the modest truth—*
what matters to me is the truth. Nothing more, nothing less.

Cinthia: *Be better suited.*
These weeds are memories of those worser hours.
I prithee, put them off.

Steve: "Be better suited. These weeds –". You're looking at her clothes –

Cinthia: Oh. Dress better!

Steve: Yes, but sympathetically. She just came up to you all messed up, but she brought you the King safely. She's been through a lot of stuff. You're saying, "Oh man, why don't we hook you up with some nicer clothes?" When you say these weeds are memories of worser hours you're saying –

Cinthia: That's what happened in the bad times.

Steve: Right. So, "These clothes are memories of those horrible—dirty things. These clothes are memories of the past." Sometimes the simplest choice is the most powerful.

Cinthia: *So please take them off.*

Marlene: They might laugh.

Steve: Let them. We're here to entertain them.

Cinthia: The way I'm going to say it, they'll understand.

Marlene: *Pardon, dear madam.*
Yet to be known shortens my made intent.
My boon I make it, that you know me not
Til time and I think it meet.

Steve: What do you think you're saying? She says change your clothes and you say, Pardon me dear madam, "yet to be known, shortens my main intent." I make it that you know me not til time and I think it meet.

Marlene: I'm still in disguise.

Steve: Yes. They shouldn't know me until I'm ready. Put it in your own words.

Marlene: *I'm still in disguise, as you can see.* —

Steve: "Pretend you don't know me." Something like that?

Marlene: *Pretend you don't know me until I tell you.*

Steve: "Until I'm ready to show myself."

Cinthia: *Say no more. How is that man?*

Steve: That could be confusing to the audience. Say something more specific.

Marlene: *How is my Lord?*

Steve: "How is my father?"
Then the doctor is going to say –. We'll wait for him.

Marlene: He'll be talking in Spanish. We have to translate.

Steve: No. We can just say it in Spanish. You understand it, right? And if you need to say something to him, you say it in Spanish. How's that? Then that's back and forth.

Cinthia: I'm talking to *him*?

Steve: It does seem like that because he's answering you.

Cinthia: Do I know he's a doctor?

Steve: Yes. We'll put him in a white coat. He'll have a little stethoscope.

Cinthia: Do I know Lear is my father?

Steve: Yes. They told you what he's been through. In the next line you'll see you pray to the gods to cure what's wrong with him. You understand that he's lost his mind and is falling apart. He might be on the point of dying.

Cinthia: *Como esta mi papa?*

Steve: Is that right, Marlene?

Marlene: *Como esta mi padre?*

Cinthia: *Oh you kind gods.*

> *Cure this great breech in his abused nature.*
> *The untuned and jarring senses. Oh, wind up*
> *Of this child-changed father.*

Steve: You're basically praying for him to be healed. *This breech in his abused nature.* This rip—heal up this damage. Something like that. Put it however you want as long as it's really passionate.

Cinthia: *Oh god,*

Please cure this great king, the great pain to his abused nature.

Then what's this?

Steve: It's the same thing. Take all the damage that's been done to him. You could cut it. It's repetitious.

Cinthia: *Fix every part of him.*

Steve: Why don't you add, "That's been destroyed."

Cinthia: Then I can cut out the last line?

Steve: Yes. The doctor will say in Spanish, "So please your majesty
That we may wake the king. He hath slept long."
He's saying, if you want, we can go wake him up.

Cinthia: *Be governed by your knowledge and proceed*
I' —?

Steve: I' apostrophe means "in."

Cinthia: *In the sway of your own will. Is he arrayed?*

Steve: Is he dressed? You're saying "Be governed by your knowledge." What does that mean?

Cinthia: Do what you—

Steve: You're saying he's the expert, he should do what he thinks is right.

Cinthia: *Do what your conscience tells you.*
Why about the clothes? Why does that matter?

Steve: Do you want to cut that about the clothes? For some reason, you're into how people look.

Cinthia: *Make sure he's dressed.*

Steve: I don't think it's a superficial concern. I don't think it's just about fashion. Why are you so concerned that he be dressed?

Cinthia: If he had all this power then he should be proper.

Steve: You're concerned that people should look the way they are inside. They should represent themselves well. Then the Gentleman's speech, the doctor could take some of that. I meant to cut the Gentleman.

(At this point Albert Young who had played Laertes in *Hamlet* dropped in.) Albert, are you realistic about wanting to take on a significant role in this? Is that something you truly will be able to do? Very serious role. I was thinking of you as the brother, the bastard. It's a fantastic part. You're trying to get your revenge and you trick your father. Really evil. You never played a really evil part. It would be another stretch for you. Very exciting. Manipulation, scheming, seduction. You are a player with both Doris and Michele.

Cinthia: They kill each other over you.

Steve: Want to do it, Albert? Very exciting. It's one of the great parts. He feels the whole world is against him and it's time for him to get justice. Then he does all these horrible things and at the end he dies and says, "What have I done?"

Albert: . . . sure!

Steve: Good choice. Let's keep going, here.

So the doctor says in Spanish, *Be by good madam, when we do awake him, I doubt not of his temperance.*

Maybe he means step aside. Be there. He's going to be confused. You can help him. It's going to be hard for him. You want to answer him in Spanish?

Marlene: "Tabien."

Steve: How do you spell that?

Marlene: T-a-b-i-e-n.

Steve: Then he says, *Please, you draw near. Louder the music there.*

They're playing music. Soothing music.

Cinthia: *Oh my dear father, restoration hang*
Thy medicine on my lips. And let this kiss
Repair those violent harms that my two sisters
Have on thy reverence made.

Steve: What are you saying?

Cinthia: *Oh my dear father*—I'm going to say that.

Steve: "Restoration hang thy medicine on my lips." Restoration is recovery. You're saying give my lips the power to heal you.

Cinthia: *Let this kiss repair the harms that my two sisters have done to you.*

Steve: Good. Go ahead.

Marlene: *Kind and dear princess.*

Steve: Yes. You're admiring her. (To Cinthia) Do you like hearing that—"kind and dear princess?"

Cinthia: Yes.

Steve: It seems to me this is a very kind and gentle moment.

Cinthia: I *am* his princess. I am the only person that cares about him. And even if I didn't want to go Shakespeare and go all out to tell you how I feel, I stuck to you and look what they did to you. You pressured them and— you know what I mean?

Steve: Good. Go again.

Cinthia: *Oh my God –*

Steve: Read it first.

Cinthia: *Had you not been their father, these white flakes—* are you not their father?

Steve: Hold on. Let's understand it first. It's not quite ready.

Cinthia: *Had you not been their father, these white flakes Did challenge pity of them.*

Steve: What are you saying?

Cinthia: You're their father and look what they did to you.

Steve: It's specifically saying that even if you weren't their father, "these white flakes"—I assume it's the hair and the beard—your age, they should have respected you just as a man who reached that age.

Cinthia: I'm angry.

Steve: You are angry and you are also pitying him and sad for what's happened.

Cinthia: *Was this a face to be opposed Against the warring winds?*

Steve: I love that line. When he's out exposed and homeless—

Cinthia: *To stand against the deep dread-bolted thunder?*
In the most terrible and nimble stroke
Of quick cross lightening to watch –"

Steve: He had to survive a storm. They kicked him out.

Cinthia: *To watch, poor perdu.*

Steve: That means, "Lost one".

Cinthia: *With this thin helm.*

Steve: His head. His hair. He had no cover.

Cinthia: *Mine enemy's dog,*
Though he had bit me, should have stood that night
Against my fire. And wast thou fain, poor father,
To hovel thee with swine

Steve: Pigs—

Cinthia: *and rogues*

Steve: Rough characters –

Cinthia: *forlorn*

Steve: Lost.

Cinthia: *by short and musty straw? Alack, Alack."*

Steve: So what you're saying is even my enemy's dog, if he bit me, could have stayed by my fire that night it was so terrible.

Cinthia: *Even my enemy's dog,*
Though he had bit me, should have stood against—

Steve: "Against" means "near". Fire means comfort on a cold and stormy night.

You're saying you had to spend the night with pigs and a bunch of lost lunatics and sleep on straw. You don't need that part but –

Cinthia: *And my father, the king,*
   Slept in the street with rats and roaches –

Steve: What about the crazy people?

Cinthia: What crazy people?

Steve: The rogues.

Cinthia: *The rats, the roaches <u>and winos</u>.* How do you spell winos?

Steve: W-i-n-o-s.

Cinthia: *Alack, alack.*

Steve: It might be good to say that because there really is no substitute for that now.

Cinthia: I'll keep one "Alack" and change the other to "Oh, my God".

Steve: "Tis wonder that thy life and wits at once Had not concluded all."

Cinthia: *Tis wonder that thy life had not concluded.*

Steve: I'm amazed that you didn't lose your mind and your life.

Cinthia: *Oh my God, having been through all this, I can't believe—*

Steve: How about, "I can't believe" and then whoosh—he wakes. What do you think of that?

Cinthia: *I can't believe—he wakes. He wakes!*

Steve: The doctor says, "Madam do you, 'tis fittest."

Cinthia: *How does my royal lord? How fares your Majesty?*

Steve: Make this as personal as you want. Both of those mean, "How are you doing?" You want to add "father"?

Cinthia: *How is my wonder, my father, my life?*

Steve: Beautiful.
> *You do me wrong to take me out of the grave.*

What does he think? He thinks he's dead. That you are a soul in heaven.
> *But I am bound*
> *Upon a wheel of fire, that mine own tears*
> *Do scold like molten lead.*

Amazing speech. He's saying you're doing the wrong thing to bring him back from the dead. He thinks you're an angel—a soul in bliss. It's so hot where I am, in my guilt that my tears are burning like molten lead.

Cinthia: *Father, you don't know who I am.*

Steve: This play, I read it almost once a year and I have to say that every passing year in my life it deepens, gets sadder and sadder. A teacher of mine in high school told me that. He said, "You'll read this for the rest of your life and like no other play or story it will make your heart ache and you'll realize the wisdom of it."

He's saying, "I never knew people suffered like this. I've been king and I never knew." He's just begging heaven saying "make the world bearable." He's been a rich kid. A child his whole life until his last days when he finally becomes an adult and he dies.

All right, so I say, *You are a spirit. When did you die?*

Cinthia: *Chill! Chill!*

Steve: That's great! Then the doctor says in Spanish, "He's scarce awake, let him alone." Take it easy on him. And the king says, *Where have I been? Where am I? Fair daylight?*

I'm going to change that to *Is this day light? I know not what to say.*
I will not swear these are my hands.
He doesn't even believe he exists.
Let's see.
I feel this pin prick.

Cinthia: *Oh, look at me.*

Steve: It's more like pleading.

Cinthia: *Look at me, dammit!*

Steve: Fine. You're saying, "Snap out of it, dad."

Cinthia: *And hold my hand in benediction —-*

Steve: That means. "Bless me," but you can change it. 'Hold *my* hand." I like that. Then it's about your relationship. Father and daughter. He's trying to kneel. I want to cut that. I don't like that kneeling stuff. It's kind of dated. What you're getting at is much more intimate. "Look at me, dammit. Hold my hand!"
Pray do not mock me.
I am a very foolish fond old man.
And to deal plainly,
I fear I am not in my perfect mind.
Oh, what a feeling to think you are losing your mind.

Pray. do not laugh at me,
For as I am a man, I think this lady to be my child
Cordelia.
I'm going to change "pray" to "please".
I'm going to cut the "fond." We don't know what fond means there.
The f-f-f is nice. *Foolish frail and to speak plainly,*
I fear I am not in my perfect mind.

Cinthia: *I am! I am!*

Steve: *Be your tears wet?*
    I'm going to say, *Are your tears wet?*

Cinthia: *Nooo!*

Steve: I'll reach up and touch your face.
    Please, don't cry.
    If you have poison for me, I will drink it.
    I know you do not love me; for your sisters
    Have, as I do remember, done me wrong.
    You have some cause, they have not.

Cinthia: What? I have the cause for you crying?

Steve: No. You have the reason because of what I did to you. I threw you out. I'm going to keep that. I think it's very clear.

Cinthia: *Not really.*

Steve: Not really? Oh, you're saying your line. And the doctor comes and says, "the great rage is killed in him." He's not angry anymore. He's not like a dangerous lunatic. And yet it's dangerous to make him go over the time he has lost. The bad memories. He's saying to you, "Let's not talk about his past because it's going to get him upset. And hurt him. Desire him to go in. "Trouble him no more."

Cinthia: *Get out of my face. You're talking about my father!*

Steve: No. More polite than that in this case. The doctor's saying encourage him to go inside. Let's keep him quiet.

Cinthia: *Will it please your highness walk?*

Steve: You're asking me.

Cinthia: *Please, father, walk with me.*

Steve: I love that. That rivals the simple power of these other lines. "Please, father, walk with me." That's beautiful. And I say *You must bear with me. Pray you now, forget and forgive. I am old and foolish.*

Cinthia: *No, you're not!*

Steve: You want to add that? "No, you're not!" Or do you want to leave it at that and we walk out together?

Cinthia: "I am old and foolish" and I let him think that? (She writes.)

Steve: She needs to be strong to make that statement.

Cinthia: *I've –*

Steve: It's like your tough love. "I don't want to hear that shit out of you."

Cinthia: *I've forgiven and forgotten a long time ago.*

Steve: Great! This guy is depressed. He's putting himself down.

Cinthia: *Don't tell me that. And walk with me!*

Steve: Yes. Get tough with the old man because he's kidding himself a lot, too. And in the beginning he's very childish. And some of it he has coming to him. Not the extremes, but some of it.

Cordelia can be a wimpy part, but this is not a wimpy Cordelia. She's the one who has courage. She's the tough one. "Stop believing that you're foolish and walk with me!" Yank me along. I know that's sometime how I am with my parents. I'll get frustrated sometimes and—not that I don't understand and sympathize, but I'll say, "Come on Dad, you know!" Children don't want to see their parents feel bad. It hurts. So you're saying, "Come on. That's not you."

Cinthia: Back up. I want to change something.
Had you not been their father,
These white flakes did challenge pity of them.

Steve: The literal meaning is that even if he were not their father, they should have respected him because of his age. You put it however you want, but that's the literal meaning.

Marlene: Should I still be here?

Steve: The audience will be very attentive to the one who is not saying anything. Once we act it out, you're a witness and it's very important there be a witness. So you're very important.

Cinthia: *Had not you been there*—I'm changing to *Even if you weren't.*

Steve: "Even if you were not there for them." Is that what you're saying?

Cinthia: *Had you not been their father, even if you weren't –*

Steve: Even if you weren't they should have respected you. I love the next and request you leave it.
"Was this a face to be opposed against the warring winds?"

Cinthia: *Is this*—isn't she looking at his face?

Steve: OK. It's in the present.
"Is this a face to be opposed against the warring winds?"

Cinthia: *To stand against the deep dread bolted thunder*
In the most terrible –

Steve: "nimble stroke of quick cross lightning to watch."
It is repetitive. If you don't want to put thunder and lightning you can stop at the warring wind.

Cinthia: *To watch—*

Steve: You went through all this without any covering, but I think we get that with the face. How could anyone expose this to that? Can we cut to "to watch, poor perdu."
Let's read the scene.

Cinthia: : *"Even if my enemy's dog had bit me,*
He would have stood that night –

Steve: Good!. Good change. He would have stood that night by my fire. One time through and then we're done.

Cinthia: (to Kent) *How shall I live and work*
To match your goodness? My life would be too short
And every measure would fail me.

Marlene: *To be acknowledged madam is to be o'erpaid.*
What matters to me is you, nothing more, nothing less.

Cinthia: *You should be able to dress better.*
These clothes are memories of the past.
Please, take them off.

Steve: (As Doctor) *So please your majesty, that we may wake the king.*
He hath slept long. Be by good madam when we do wake him.
I doubt not of his temperance.
Please you, draw near.
Louder the music there.

Cinthia: *Oh my dear father. Let this kiss restore the harm my two sisters have done to you.*

Marlene: *Kind and dear Princess.*

Cinthia: *Had you not been their father? Even if you weren't,*
They should have respected you. Is this a face to be opposed
against the warring winds?
Even if my enemy's dog had bit me
He would have stood there that night by the fire.
And my father, the king, slept in the streets with rats, roaches and winos.
Alack, oh my God. Having been through all this, I can't believe –
He wakes! Speak to him."

Steve: (As doctor) *Do you. 'tis fittest.*

Cinthia: *How is my life? My father?*

Steve: *You do me wrong to take me out of the grave.*
You are a soul in bliss. But I am bound
Upon a wheel of fire that mine own tears
Do scald like molten lead.

Cinthia: *Father, do you know me?*

Steve: *You are a spirit, I know. When did you die?*

Cinthia: *Chill! Chill! Back up!*

Steve: (as Doctor) *He's scarce awake. Let him alone a while.*
(as Lear) *Where have I been? Where am I? Is this daylight?*
I know not what to say. I will not swear these are my hands.
Let's see. I feel this pin prick.

Cinthia: *Look at me, dammit and hold my hand.*

Steve: *Do not mock me. I am a very foolish, frail old man.*
And to speak plainly, I fear I am not in my perfect mind.
Do not laugh at me for as I am a man
I think this lady to be my child Cordelia.

Cinthia: *I am.*

Steve: *Are your tears wet? Yes.*
Please, don't cry. If you have poison for me, I will drink it. I know you do not love me. Your sisters, as I do remember, have done me wrong.
You have some cause, they have not.

Cinthia: *Not really.*

Steve: (as Doctor) *Be comforted, good madam. The great rage you see is killed in him and yet it is danger to make him even o'er the time he has lost.*
Desire him to go in. Trouble him no more
Till further settling.

Cinthia: *Please father, look at me.*

Steve: *You must bear with me. Forget and forgive. I am old and foolish.*

Cinthia: *I have forgiven and forgotten a long time ago. Now stop believing that you are foolish and walk with me!*

Steve: Yes!!! Excellent! Beautiful, really. It's a beautiful scene. Terrific. That's all for today.

(After having left his teaching job to devote full attention to Real People Theatre, Stephen Haff left the company in 2004 to return to his home in Canada. As this book goes to press, the company is seeking to continue without him and working to raise money to keep its rented space.)

Hobart Shakespeareans

The Fool in *King Lear*

Rafe Esquith set forth his approach to teaching in his book *There Are No Shortcuts* published by Pantheon books in 2003, ISBN: 0-375-42202-1. A google search reveals a great deal of material about Esquith's work with the Hobart Shakespeareans, the foundation he has set up for it, and the commendations he has received. Contact information:

>Rafe Esquith
>Hobart Elementary
>Hobart Shakespeareans
>980 South Hobart Boulevard
>Los Angeles, CA 90006
>Phone: 213 200-4700
>e-mail: willpower6@aol.com

Program Cover, Shakespeare & Company Fall Festival 2003

Shakespeare & Company

A beautiful formulation of the reasons for doing Shakespeare is found in the following statement that appeared in the Twenty-Fifth Anniversary Program of Shakespeare & Company in 2002.

Shakespeare & Company
Mission, Vision, Values

We value the pursuit of excellence and work to feel pride and pleasure in all of our endeavors. Founded in 1978, Shakespeare & Company aspires to create a theatre of unprecedented excellence rooted in the classical ideals of inquiry, balance and harmony; a company that performs as the Elizabethans did—in love with poetry, physical prowess, and the mysteries of the universe. With a core of over 120 artists, the Company performs Shakespeare, generating opportunities for collaboration between actors, directors and designers of all races, nationalities and backgrounds. Shakespeare & Company provides original, in-depth, classical training and performance methods. Shakespeare & Company also develops and produces new plays of political and social significance. Shakespeare and Company's education programs inspire a new generation of students and scholars to discover the resonance of Shakespeare's truths in the everyday world, demonstrating the influence that classical theatre can have within a community.

Statement of Vision

To establish a theatre company which, by its commitment to the creative impulse, is a revolutionary force in society, which connects the truths of the past to the challenges and possibilities of today, which finds it source in the performance of Shakespeare's plays, and teaches the widest possible audience through training and education as well as performance.

A Statement of the Values the Unite Us

Under all Shakespeare's plays are three vital questions:
What does it mean to be alive?
How should we act?
What must I do?
By making the performance and exploration of Shakespeare's plays the center of our lives, it follows as the night day that we must ask ourselves these questions in all our actions. The plays themselves demand that we take ourselves out into the social and political fields, making connections between the arts and humanities, arts and government, arts and business, arts and education, arts and spirituality.

Shakespeare & Company is made up of activities in the following areas: Performance, Training, Education, Management, Academia/Research, Development/Entrepreneurism, Architecture, Landscaping and Gardening.

Shakespeare & Company is generated out of the classical principles present in the experience of performing and producing Shakespeare's plays. These classical principles are the foundation upon which all programs and activities are built.

By classical, we mean: "the highest truths told in a universally accessible form which have an impact that is healing for the individual and society."

The ethic and aesthetic of the following commonly-held values and beliefs identify and unify this Company. These values and beliefs help to align us with classical principles:

We believe that the creative impulse is essential to the human soul, and that the Arts are the most realized expression of this impulse.

We believe that the ultimate pursuit and practice of Art creates values that are compassionate and humane.

The symbiosis of performance, training, education, and management creates a clarity and deepening of experience critical to a healthy company and enhances the creative impulse.

We believe that participating in the community where we live both enriches our lives and the quality of out work. We strive to be good neighbors.

We value a society in which peoples of all races and ethnicity live with mutual respect, generosity, interest in, and commitment to the greater good of all. We continually strive to have this value reflected in the makeup of our Company.

We believe that while working for an arts organization is a privilege and has its own rewards, our employees should receive competitive wages and secure benefits.

We believe in a mentoring model that both educates and transmits values, and that this model is essential to the health of this Company as well as society.

We value open and honest communication and strive to implement it on every level, even when it is difficult or unpleasant.

We value the exercise of wit and humor to leaven our interactions with ourselves and others. We believe in playfulness and grace in all our actions.

We value the pursuit of excellence, and work to feel pride and pleasure in all of our endeavors.

>Shakespeare & Company
>72 Kemble Street
>Lenox, MA 01240-2813
>413 637-1199
>**http://www.shakespeare.org**
>e-mail: general@shakespeare.org

ENDNOTES

[i] Darcy Frey, *The Last Shot: City Streets, Basketball Dreams* (New York: Mariner Books, 2004).

[ii] Lois Burdett, *A Child's Portrait of Shakespeare* (Buffalo, New York: Firefly Books (U.S.) 1995. The book is illustrated by Burdett's students and there are examples of their writing. Rhyming couplet versions of *Twelfth Night, Macbeth, A Midsummer Night's Dream, Romeo and Juliet, The Tempest, Hamlet,* and *Much Ado about Nothing* are available in the same series, all illustrated by the students. Examples of their writing is included.

[iii] Lois Burdett phone interview with the author, September 22, 2002.

[iv] Stephen Haff phone interview with the author, July 3, 2002.

[v] Rafe Esquith, *There Are No Shortcuts* (New York: Pantheon Books, 2003).

[vi] Rafe Esquith phone interview with the author, July 6, 2003.

[vii] *Shakespeare & Company 25 Years* (Lenox, MA), 2002 Program, 4.

[viii] Kevin Coleman, interview with the author , Lenox, MA, October 20 2002.

[ix] Cinthia Candeleria, interview with the author at Bushwick High School, Brooklyn, New York, October 24, 2002

[x] Mary Hartman, interview with the author, Lenox, MA, Dec 13, 2002.

[xi] Brian Mason interview with the author, Lenox, MA, November 20, 2003.

xii Michael Wood, *Shakespeare* (New York: Basic Books, 2003).

xiii Garry O'Connor, *William Shakespeare: A Popular Life* (New York: Applause, 2000).

xiv The author had the good fortune, although it did not always feel like it at the time, to have Kazan lead discussions after parts of two of the author's plays were presented at the Actor's Studio Playwrights' Unit in New York in the 1950's.

xv Jan Kott, Shakespeare our Contemporary. (Translated from the Polish by Boleslaw Taborski) (New York: Doubleday, 1964).

xvi Peter Hall, "Shakespeare and the Modern Director," in *Royal Shakespeare Theatre Company 1960-63 in Stratford-on-Avon and London*, (London: Max Reinhardt, 1964), pp. 41, 42.

xvii Paul Sugarman, *Passport to Shakespeare: The Raw Shakespeare Approach to Shakespeare for Everyone* (Bloomfield, NJ : Puck Press, 2003), p. 7.

xviii The RawShakespeare Pocket Editions, (Bloomfield, NJ) are not annotated. The Applause First Folio Editions (New York: Applause Books, 1997), are annotated. Both are available in paper editions.

xix Kelly Teahen, "Playing Macbeth, A Step into the Dark," *Fanfares A Publication for Members of the Stratford Festival of Canada*, Spring 2004, p. 8.

xx Ralph Berry, *On Directing Shakespeare: Interviews with Contemporary Directors* (London: Hamish Hamilton, 1989), p. 75.

xxi Brian Mason interview.

xxii The author had the opportunity to participate in Littlewood's workshops for her production of *The Projector* at the Theatre Royal at Stratford E. 15 in London, England, February 1970.

xxiii Mason interview.

[xxiv] Gaye Brown, interview with the author, January 14, 1970, Theatre Royal (Stratford) London.

[xxv] Robert Sugarman *Circus for Everyone: Circus Learning Around the World* (Shaftsbury, VT : Mountainside Press, 2001) p. 21.

[xxvi] Eric Partridge, *Shakespeare's Bawdy* (London & New York: Routledge, 2001).

[xxvii] Rafe Esquith, phone interview with the author. January 25, 2004.

[xxviii] Kevin Coleman interview with the author, Lenox, MA. May 3, 2004.

[xxix] Peter Brook, *The Empty Space* (London: McGibbon, & Kee, 1968). p. 115.

[xxx] Eric Bagai *Eric@foreworks.com*, Email "Sad Clowning and Teens" March 1, 2004

[xxxi] Garry O'Connor, *William Shakespeare: A Popular Life* (New York: Applause, 2000), p. 210.

BIBLIOGRAPHY

BOOKS

Esquith, Rafe. *There are no Shortcuts*. New York, NY: Pantheon, 2003.

Shakespeare, His World, His Stage

Beckerman, Bernard. *Shakespeare at the Globe 1599-1609*. New York, NY: Macmillan, 1962.

De Banke, Cecily. *Shakespearean Stage Production*. London, UK: Hutchinson, 1954.

Freeman, Neil. *The Applause First Folio of Shakespeare in Modern Type* (One volume collection of 36 plays). New York, NY: Applause, 2001

Greenblatt, Stephen. *Will in the World*. New York, NY: Norton, 2004

Gurr, Andrew and John Orrell. *Rebuilding Shakespeare's Globe* with a Foreword by Sam Wanamaker. London, UK: Weidenfeld and Nicolson, 1989.

Nagler, A.W.. *Shakespeare's Stage*. New Haven, CT: Yale UP., 1958.

O'Connor, Garry. *Shakespeare: A Popular Life*, New York, NY: Applause, 1999.

Onions, C.T.. *A Shakespeare Glossary*, New York, NY: Oxford Univ. Press, 1986.

Partridge, Eric. *Shakespeare's Bawdy*. New York, NY: Routledge, 3rd Edition, 1968.

Spurgeon, Caroline F.E.. *Shakespeare's Imagery*. Boston, MA: Beacon, 1958.

Tillyard, E.M.W.. *The Elizabethan World Picture*. New York, NY: Random House.

Tucker, Patrick. *Secrets of Acting Shakespeare*. New York, NY: Routledge, 2002

Wood, Michael. *Shakespeare*. New York, NY: Basic Books, 2003.

Shakespeare Today

Berry, Ralph. *On Directing Shakespeare*. London, UK: Penguin, 1989.

Brown, John Russell. *Shakespeare's Plays in Performance*, new and revised. New York, NY: Applause, 1993.

Kott, Jan. *Shakespeare our Contemporary*. Garden City, NY: Doubleday, 1964.

Acting/Directing

Berry, Cicely. *The Actor and the Text*. New York, NY: Applause, 1992.

Clurman, Harold. *On Directing*. New York, NY: Fireside, 1997.

Hagen, Uta. *Respect for Acting*. New York, NY: Macmillan, 1973

Linklater, Kristin. *Freeing Shakespeare's Voice: The Actor's Guide to Speaking the Text*. New York, NY: Theatre Communication Group, 1992.

Smith, David. *The East/West Exercise Book*. New York, NY: McGraw-Hill, 1976.

Spolin, Viola. *Improvisation for the Theater*. Evanston, IL: Northwestern University Press, 1963.

Stanislavski, Konstantin. *Building a Character*. New York, NY: Theatre Arts, 1949.

Suzman, Janet. *Acting with Shakespeare: The Comedies*. New York, NY: Applause, 1996.

Texts

There are many fine paperback editions of Shakespeare's plays. They include:

Freeman, Neil. *Applause First Folio Editions* (individual plays). New York, NY: Applause.

Brown, John Russell. *The Applause Shakespeare Library* (individual plays, annotated). New York, NY: Applause.

The Raw Shakespeare Pocket Editions of the First Folio Settings. Bloomfield, NJ: Puck Press.

Adaptations

Burdett, Lois. *Shakespeare Can Be Fun*. Rhymed adaptations of many of the plays published individually. Art work by the second grade students who performed them. Suggestions for activities. Willowdale, Ontario, Canada: Firefly Books.

Hall-Schor, Catharine. *Young People's Shakespeare Series*. One hour versions of *A Winter's Tale, A Midsummer Night's Dream* and *The Tempest* that have been performed in grammar schools. Production suggestions. Shaftsbury, VT: Mountainside Press.

Background Materials for Young People and their Directors

Aagesen, Colleen and Margie Blumberg. *Shakespeare for Kids: His Life and Times. 21 Activities.* Chicago, IL: Chicago Review Press, 1999.

Burson, Linda. *Play with Shakespeare.* Charlottesville, NC: New Play Books, 1992. Games, activities and four short adaptations.

DVD/VIDEO:

Michele Chayon, dir. *Colors Straight Up.* Echo Pictures, 1997.

An account of a theatre program with high schoolers in the Watts section of Los Angeles.

Beaubien, dir. *The Secret of Will: One Grade 2 Class + William Shakespeare = A Journey of a Lifetime.* Toronto, Ontario, Canada: Twelfth Night Films, 2002

A record of Lois Burdett's second grade class.

INDEX

52nd St. Project, 37
Aaron (char.), 5
American Theatre, 37
Angels in America, 69
As You Like It, 83, 104
Bach, 17
Bagai, Eric, 110
Beethoven, 17
Bennington College, 36, 137
Black Plague, The, 31
Bottom (char.), 78, 109, 111, 120-121, 124-126
Branagh, Kenneth, 23, 90, 135
Burdett, Lois, *xi*, *xiv*, 2, 7-8, 11-12, 17, 27-29, 63-64, 76-77, 135-136
Burton, Richard, 23
Camelot, 88
Candeleria, Cinthia, 33, 38, 136, 138
Celia (char.), 62
Chaplin, Charlie, 100
Character Freezes, 61
Child's Portrait of Shakespeare, A, 33, 135
Claudio (char.), 14
Cobweb (char.), 124
Cohn, Roy (char.), 69
Coleman, Kevin, *xi*, *xiv*, 2, 24, 52, 76, 92, 95
Cordelia (char.), 33, 38-40, 102, 107, 138-140, 151, 153, 156
Creating the World, 62
Day for Night, 112
Demetrius (char.), 16, 32, 101, 107-109, 116-117, 119-124, 126
Dogberry (char.), 109
Egeus (char.), 107-108, 126-127
Ellison, Caitlin, 134
Esquith, Rafe, *xi*, *xiv*, 7-8, 21, 27, 41, 63, 71, 73, 76-77, 80, 84-85, 88-90, 94-95, 107, 157, 167
Fall Festival, 2, 25, 53, 77, 87, 158
Feeding In, 61, 79, 83, 106
Feore, Colm, 102
Fiddler on the Roof, 13
Flute (char.), 78, 111
Fontanne, Lynne, 94
Founders Theatre, 25, 53, 77
Globe Theatre, The, 18, 46, 76
Gray, Wallace, 72
Grock, 110

171

172 *Index*

Guinness, Alec, 11
Guthrie, Tyrone, 11
Haff, Stephen, *xi, xiv,* 7-8, 18, 21, 27, 33, 35, 37-40, 63, 72, 75-76, 79, 82, 138-156
Hall, Peter, 46, 73
Hall-Schor, Catharine, *xiv,* 169
Hamlet School, *xiv,* 2, 28
Hamlet, 2, 12, 19-23, 34-36, 38, 44, 57, 77, 90-91, 106, 114, 135, 137, 144
Hamlet (char.), 35, 43-44, 53, 69, 90-91, 107
Hamnet, 31
Hartman, Mary, *xiv,* 24, 55, 78, 133
Hathaway, Anne, 18
Hermia (char.), 28, 32, 78, 101, 103, 107-109, 116, 118-124, 126
Hiland Hall School, 0
Hippolyta (char.), 27-28, 101, 103-106, 109, 113, 125-127
Hobart Elementary School, 2, 21, 41
Hobart Shakespeareans, *xiv,* 21-22, 27, 41, 45-46, 49, 157
Hunt, Matt, 29
Iago (char.), 5

Instant Shakespeare Company, 73-74, 95
Irwin, Bill, 100
It Takes a Classroom to Do a Monologue, 53, 105
Jones, Sophie, 29
Juliet (char.), 53, 61, 72, 82, 102, 107
Kander and Ebb, 83
Kate (char.), 102, 115
Kazan, Elia, *xiv,* 69, 94
Keaton, Buster, 100
King Lear, 5, 38, 84, 93, 100, 102, 137-138, 157
King Lear (char.), 14, 40, 69, 102, 138-156
Kott, Jan, 73, 168
Kushner, Tony, 69
Larrible, David, 110
Laurel and Hardy, 100-101
Leontes (char.), 14
Literal Meaning, 59, 82, 153
Littlewood, Joan, *xiv,* 79, 84, 94, 106
Loman, Willy (char.), 69
Los Angeles, 2, 7, 21, 41, 137, 157, 170
Lubin, Barry, 110
Lugo, Marlene, 33, 40, 136, 138
Lunt, Alfred, 94
Lysander (char.), 32, 101, 107-109, 118-124, 126
Man and Superman, 108

McKellen, Ian, 22, 42, 45, 49, 73
Mercutio (char.), 72, 92
Midsummer Night's Dream, A, xvi, 16, 28, 57, 67, 78, 89, 99-101, 103, 106, 114, 118, 128, 135, 169
Mostel, Zero, 100
Mozart, 17
Much Ado about Nothing, 109, 135
Mustard Seed (char.), 124
New Dramatists, 37, 137
New York City, 19, 63, 73
Nock, Bello, 110
North Bennington Graded School, 0
Nurse (char.), 92
Oberon (char.), 15-16, 101, 112-125
Oh, What a Lovely War!, 84
Olivier, Laurence, 11, 23
Ophelia, 35, 54, 90-91
Othello, 5, 57
Patterson, Tom, 11
Peaseblossom, 124
Petruchio, 102, 115
Philostrate, 101, 106, 109, 127
platea, 4-5, 86, 132
Poel, William, 87
Potter, Harry, 114

Puck, 30, 32-33, 112-113, 115-117, 119-125, 128, 169
Quigley, Pat, *xiv*, 78
Quince, 111
Real People Theatre, 8, 18, 27, 136-137, 156
Richard III, 5, 11, 87, 89
Romeo (char.), 52-53, 72, 87, 102, 107
Romeo and Juliet, 13, 18, 20, 58, 60, 90, 93, 135, 137
Rosalind (char.), 62
Santiago, Doris, 138
Semple, Goldie, 102
Shakespeare & Co., *xi*, *xiv*, 2, 7-8, 21, 24-25, 27, 52-53, 55-56, 61, 63, 67, 71, 73-75, 77, 79, 86-87, 89, 92, 95, 104, 106, 109, 111, 114, 118, 137, 158-162
Shakespeare's clowns, 109
Shaw, George Bernard, 108
Sly, Christopher (char.), 124
Snowt (char.), 111
Snug (char.), 111
Starveling (char.), 111
Stratford Festival, 74, 78, 89, 104
Summer Shakespeare Academy, 0
Tanner, Jack, 108
Text Layout, 59, 60

Text out of Context, 59-60
There Are No Shortcuts, 63, 80, 157, 167
Theseus (char.), 28, 101-106, 109, 113, 125-127
Titania (char.), 43, 101, 112-118, 120-125
Titus Andronicus, 5
Troilus and Cressida, 89, 103
Utah Shakespeare Festival, 15
Wars of the Roses, 73
Woolfenden, Guy, 118
Wooster Group, The, 27, 137
Yale, 18, 37,
Youdina, Alla, 81
Young, Albert, 138, 144
Zefferelli, Franco, 23
Zoppe, Giovanni (Nino), 110
Zorba, 83

ROBERT SUGARMAN is an author and playwright. His plays have been performed across the country. His book, *Circus for Everyone: Circus Learning Around the World* was the first to chronicle the many circus training programs, amateur and professional, child and adult that have developed in recent years. Mr. Sugarman has taught at the State University of New York/Albany, Bennington College, Southern Vermont College and Cazenovia College. He has directed plays in many venues. He was a member of the Playwrights Unit at the Actors Studio in New York City and worked with director Joan Littlewood in London. He is chair of the Circus Area at the Popular Culture Association and has presented papers at the Circus Historical Society.

Also available from Mountainside Press

CIRCUS FOR EVERYONE:
Circus Learning Around the World

Robert Sugarman

Circus for Everyone: Circus Learning Around the World is the first study of the circus training programs that have emerged in the last 25 years. Programs help at-risk youth develop good work habits and self-esteem. Curricular and extracurricular programs provide non-competitive physical activity that adapts to the needs of all children. Academic programs produce professional performers.

"**All over the world people have been waiting for this book.** More and more young people are looking for a way to train themselves in a rigorous, disciplined and creative way. Robert Sugarman, in a staggering feat of research has chronicled hundreds of CIRCUS OPPORTUNITIES! Here are the names, places and telephone numbers where your dreams can come true." —**Reg Bolton**, author *Circus in a Suitcase* director, SUITCASE CIRCUS, West Australia.

"Comprehensive in scope, *Circus for Everyone* is a valuable resource for anyone involved in teaching or learning circus skills. Its Resource Guide is an indispensable resource for the kind of future communication between schools and teachers that it will certainly inspire." —**Ernest Albrecht**, author, *New American Circus*, Publisher, SPECTACLE

Photos. Geographically arranged resource guide.
288 pages. Over 50 illustrations.
ISBN: 0-9708693-0-4 • $16.95